THE LIVING MASS

THE
LIVING
MASS

BY REV. HAROLD J. WICKEY

THE BRUCE PUBLISHING COMPANY
MILWAUKEE

NIHIL OBSTAT:

    THEODORE LEUTERMAN, O.S.B.
    Censor Deputatus

IMPRIMATUR:

    ✠ EDWARD J. HUNKELER, D.D.
    Archbishop of Kansas City, Kansas
    January 19, 1960

The Scripture quotations are in the translation of Monsignor Ronald A. Knox, copyright 1944, 1948, and 1950, Sheed and Ward, Inc., New York. Permission to use the Knox translation was given by His Eminence the Cardinal Archbishop of Westminster.

Library of Congress Catalog Card Number: 61–13005

© 1961 THE BRUCE PUBLISHING COMPANY
MADE IN THE UNITED STATES OF AMERICA

Contents

Great Moments

British seashore folks pronounce it to rhyme with heaven-see. It lay low on the southern coast of England, drowsing in the sun of late September. Its small houses, tucked under their thatched roofs, gleamed in white-washed brilliance, and pendants of smoke dangled above the village, like sinuous pillars supporting the cornflower blue Sussex sky. Seaward lay the Strait of Dover; inland, the long swelling countryside, flecked with pasturing flocks and wooded copses.

Pevensey awoke in the fall of 1066 to the ring of sword out of scabbard, of shield against coat of mail. Up out of the sea drove ships crowded with young warriors brandishing long bows and crossbows, kite-shaped shields, spears, and hefty broadswords. Nervous stallions whinnied and pawed at oaken decks. Oarsmen and sailors at the tillers of stout ships sang out in rich voices as their vessels ground up on the shingly beach. A muscular soldier, first to leap into the rinse of surf, fell on the pebbly footing, but leaped gracefully to his feet with a shout, "By the splendor of God, I have taken seizin of England."

Out of the ships they came, bearded and brown, in coats and short breeches of mail, striding with their spears and glinting shields, up through the village now wide awake, along a dusty road through the downs to Hastings. Dark eyes flashed under the steel helmets as the warriors shouted and sang on their way to Hastings. North of the town, on October 14, 1066, they threw themselves fiercely at Anglo-Saxon troops massed behind locked shields on a little plateau. Two-handed battle-axes rose and fell, and the afternoon was riven by the battle sound, arrows whirring and stone hammers ringing on armor. By sunset the invading warriors rested, leaning against their tall shields, and bound up their wounds. They were the conquerors of England there in the murmuring, crickety sunset. Their leader, the man who had fallen in the surf, would be known in history as William the Conqueror. Even now he was looking through narrowed eyes at the swelling hills to the north. Beyond lay London, and the throne of England.

What they could not know was that in that wild melee of October 14, two great peoples had awakened a germ of constitutional life from which would come one of the world's most successful experiments in democracy, the United States of America. When William the Conqueror stormed Battle

2

abbey and overthrew King Harold's battle standard, there began that remarkable evolution of government, from the absolutism of the eleventh century, with all power focused in the king, to our great American democracy, with all power centered in the people. That was a great, a momentous afternoon, near Hastings.

More momentous is the half hour in which Mass is offered. It has effects far more reaching than Hastings, effects that reach beyond time and are felt in the parliament of the human heart where policy is fashioned on which immortal destiny depends. In the commonwealth of grace, the Mass shapes and guides these critical decisions, introduces Christ into the council chambers of the human will. His statesmanship directs the government of souls, on each of whom depends utterly its whole destiny. The Mass assures mankind of the "freedom of the sons of God" which outstrips anything issuing from the political crises of any age.

One day, when "modern" democracies are perhaps no more than curiosities in civics books of the interplanetary period, the Mass will still be conserving in the world the freedom and beauty of life in Christ as lived in countless human souls the world over.

When Caesar crossed the Rubicon, a great change was begun in Roman history, a change felt by millions. But it was not as great as the change in the welfare (both spiritual and temporal) of all the people on earth — and of those in purgatory and in heaven — when the consecration of the Mass takes place in a tiny mission chapel in Arizona. The Roman said with great pride. "Civis Romanus sum!" (I am a Roman citizen!) Yet we can cry with more lawful pride, "I help offer Mass, I am a co-Christian (co-Christ), actively sharing in Christ's sacrifice on the altar."

3

The Greeks of the days of Pericles (B.C. 490–429) reveled in their Hellenic heritage. Proudly they looked up to the Acropolis, where the Majestic Parthenon poised in columned splendor and the Erechtheum showed off its four porches and their great Ionic columns. Proudly they showed goggle-eyed visitors from remote provinces their Temples of Athena Nike, Zeus, Poseidon, and Apollo. This was the "golden age" of Greece. Master architects like Mnesicles, Ictinus, and Callicrates were designing symphonies in stone that helped make Athens the cultural center of the world. Philosophy was having a heyday, too. Old folks still remembered seeing melancholic, obtuse Heraclitus; Parmenides, Zeno, Anaxagoras, Leucippus of Miletus, Protagoras, Hippias, and Socrates were offering solutions to the riddle of life and reality.

Athens was flexing well-conditioned biceps. The Persians had fallen at Plataea in 479 before the seasoned Greek hoplites.

Just seven years later Aeschylus, most popular playwright in Athens, produced the *Persae*. Also gathering sheaves of immortality were the tragedians Euripides, unorthodox and misunderstood, and that chronic winner of first prizes at the festival of the Wine Press and the Greater Dionysis, Sophocles. It was certainly a "golden age." All the Greeks, or "Hellenes" as they called themselves, gloried in their neighbors' and in their country's accomplishments.

We can glory more in the supreme act of assisting at Mass. It is a human accomplishment, as well as a divine one. God alone is not sufficient for the Mass; there must be a human instrument. The Christians' greatest glory is their deputization as co-offerers of the Mass by baptism and confirmation. How proud they are of their role, for they realize that the Mass produces great designs of virtue, builds character with everlasting effects, throws up great walls around the human heart

4

to keep out besieging fear and unhappiness, fashions indescribably beautiful temples in souls where God comes to live
intimately. The Mass's beauty is one of divine mercy, nailed
to a cross, beckoning with outstretched arms to the whole
human race and inviting it to peace and union with that
Pierced Heart.

Unlike the lovely Grecian columns and "topless towers of
Ilium," the beauty of the Mass is imperishable, and so acceptable that God finds it winning and attractive because it is the
act of His Son. Truly "topless," the Mass reaches up into
heaven to gladden the saints who have profited in life from
its global power and appeal.

Each Mass heard is another large step toward self-control,
toward real Christian freedom. Freedom to do right. Hence
each time of Mass is of critical import to men, for it is a time
when the greatest tyrant of all is subjected: selfishness.

Historians savor January 27, 1649, as a milestone on the
rutted, zigzagging cowtrack toward political freedom. On that
day, Charles I of England was decapitated for trying "to over-
throw the rights and liberties of the people." How? By denying
them, as his predecessors had, a share in government. "For
the people," he said on the gibbet, "I truly desire their liberty
and freedom as much as anybody whosoever. But I must tell
you that their liberty and freedom consist in having government, those laws by which their life and their goods may be
most their own. It is not for having a share in the government,
sirs, that is nothing appertaining to them."

The executioner put his ax through its familiar, practiced
arch on that raw January day, and a king died. It was a step
toward "government of the people." A clumsy step perhaps, a
step taken by men as dictatorial in their views as Charles in
his. But a step anyhow. And as a thousand pairs of eyes gazed

5

with a curious, sorrowful fascination at the bowed figure of their king as he knelt to a well-honed blade, perhaps in their hearts flickered a spark: that *theirs* is the right to form a government, *theirs* the right to choose rulers, *theirs* the right to say how much power the rulers will have.

Self-will is a tyrant in human affairs totally lacking in benevolence, unlike Charles I. The Mass routs this ruthless ravager of character and virtue, frees the soul for service to a truly benevolent Christ, just King. Only a man himself can restore this tyrant of self-will in the kingdom of his soul, once it has been overthrown. In the 300 years since little Charles's head was lopped off, far greater tyrants have come to destroy freedom. Communism is only the latest in that dismal reckoning. What the Mass does it does for good — unless a man deliberately choose to undo it.

The Puritans who had worked so energetically for Charles's death allowed precious little freedom; in America (there were 30,000 of them in the thirteen colonies by 1650) they tolerated anything but tolerance! And Catholic emancipation did not come in England till 1829! Freedom in human affairs has come slowly and cost rivers of blood and mountains of sacrifice. Yet the Mass wins freedom in Christ in a brief lifetime.

The Mass gives invincible hope. Hope against the tyranny of Satan. The Arab fanatic rides his mare, brandishing a scimitar and thinking (as Christ predicted in the Gospel read the Sunday after Ascension) that "in killing Christ's followers he does a service to God." If his victims are martyrs, he *has* done a service to God and to them, but in a way that he did not realize or intend! In human affairs the Mass can deftly bring good out of catastrophe.

The moment of Mass is a moment of emancipation. Negroes hip-deep in cotton and tobacco fields heard, but did not at first believe, the great new "gospel": Abe Lincoln had made them free. What a great moment for them — and for us who bask in Lincoln's wisdom and courage in doing what was right, even though it cost him, when all is said and done, his life.

Yet for human dignity and truth, the moment of Mass is greater. It emancipates souls from purgatory, and these freed spirits gain not merely earthly and temporal freedom, like the freed slaves in the South (which freedom, by the way, turned out for many to be merely political and legal). But souls gain eternal and perfect freedom in every sphere of human activity, because they are given a full, direct view of God as He really is.

History is made of great moments. They are, in a sense, torches of significance which light up the commonplace realities of time and humanity and endow them with meaning and direction. They are like the lights of a great city as viewed from a speeding airliner in the night: they give shape and meaning to the darkness beneath.

The old shepherd lay dying in his tent, his children gathered about him. Old Abraham died and was buried by sons Isaac and Ismael, but he died full of faith just as he had lived. He knew that somehow, somewhere in a sudden burning tinder of time, the entire world would be blessed through his own posterity (Gen. 22:18).

Yet the moment of the Mass is an historical fact that lightens up the earth like the sun, giving meaning and purpose to all that baffles, bores, and burdens. In Abraham's death there was the promise of a blessing for the weary world; in the Mass, Christ's mystic death, there is fulfillment. There is, in fact, the very reality toward which Abraham peered across the centuries. Mary was a descendant of his, and through her the world got Jesus. The Mass contains Him, for our enjoyment and our peace. It is His act, though He lets us in on it.

Frustration often lies, the hidden barb, in every human effort. Somehow, in some time, our will must be in vain, our efforts miss hitting their target. In England in 1549, inflation made money increasingly worthless and prices soared. Men with no jobs, no fields to till, no harvests to reap, stood idly on street corners and cussed. And the government tightened up the laws on vagrancy! Out in the eastern counties a bold, energetic man named Robert Kett got popular support and set up a court to try landlords judged to be oppressing the people. "We pray," wrote Kett and his fellow insurgents in a petition, "that all bondmen be made free. For God made all free with his precious blood-shedding."

Parliament, which had refused to make laws ending the abuses of the landlords (especially those who set aside too much land for pasturage, leaving none for tillage and throwing farmers out of work), sent troops out against Kett. The uprising was crushed, Kett executed.

There was a flashing there of something precious, that the hired thugs of the Earl of Warwick could not douse: the dignity of man, his eternal cry for freedom. It was the same cry the French peasants uttered in the desperate, sultry summer of 1789, as they attacked the *chateaux* of the nobility and ransacked monasteries and palaces of bishops. Kett and his farmers augured what was to come to despots. From France to Ghana the cry for freedom has thrilled the hearts of men. The Mass is for men who want to be free. The Mass is for men who will be slaves to no one.

Sometimes destiny plays out her epic role on a heroic stage with whole nations massed in the gallery breathlessly watching. Such was Sunday morning July 14, 1918. From midnight till four in the morning night-clubbing Parisians could hear the faint thunder of heavy artillery out beyond Chateau-Thierry and Dormans. At four a.m. the Germans began their *Friedensturm*. Objective: Rheims. World War I hung in the balance. "If my offensive at Rheims succeeds," said Ludendorff, "we have won the war." Said Marshall Foch grimly, "If the German attack at Rheims succeeds, we have lost the war." Across the Marne poured the allied forces in the ghostly dawn, and across three miles of burned and blasted earth in the Province of Champagne the ugly issues of war were exchanged. Italian, French, and American doughboys threw Ludendorff back. Rheims was saved. The war was won.

In the no-man's land of consciousness, a war is waged between good and evil, the old man and the new. The Mass is the supply line, bringing up reinforcements of inspiration and strength for victory. On the cross Christ wrestled with evil for the souls of men. Human weakness and human need are satisfied on the cross, hence in the Mass. Men were saved on the cross. Men are saved in the Mass.

Its forces are devastating. We gasp to remember that 60 per cent of Hiroshima was destroyed by a single atomic bomb on August 6, 1945. Still we recall the gaunt twisted skeletons of steel standing grotesquely in the deep rubble. "A rain of ruin from the air," said then President Harry Truman, "the like of which has never been seen on this earth." Great moments in history — full of tragedy and sorrow, portentous.

The Mass destroys too, but only what is evil, namely the city of sin. There is no mushrooming cloud attached to the Mass — unless perhaps the billowing incense at a Solemn Mass. But there is enormous power there, destructive of sin and capable of restoring sanity and harmony to a driven, harassed, zany, intractable, determined world. The power of damage modern weapons possess is staggering to the imagination. No more can we estimate the good done and joy assured by the

Mass, God's H-bomb of spiritual power. The "shock waves" reaching out from the altar of sacrifice have jarred countless sinners out of their lassitude or indifference, the mediocre and self-assured out of their complacency, the timid out of their fear.

The Mass builds. Because to destroy sin is to build virtue, to destroy evil is to build good. And it takes far greater power and wisdom to build. Recently I watched a wrecking crew demolish an old apartment building to make room for a new university dormitory. In came the workmen with sledges and crowbars and heavy equipment, and in a few days the apartment was razed to the ground. Then came the skilled workmen, and they proceeded to put up a beautiful five-story structure that was expressive of man's genius and good taste.

The Mass doesn't merely demolish vice; it builds a palace inside a man fit for the Holy Trinity to live in on a permanent basis. God takes a long-term lease on our soul which only we ourselves can terminate. No wonder at the Consecration heads are bowed with gratitude, fingers lightly beat breasts in astonishment and humility at this thought: God incarnates His divine Son and His infinite ability to put us right in each holy Mass. In a half hour, attending Mass, we are made richer than oil barons, we become the true nobility of earth, worth the death and body and blood of God.

A Debt to Pay

THE death of Jesus Christ on the cross was not just a nice gesture. Fastened to the wood, our Lord did not say to His Father, "Here is a small *gift* for you, my redemptive death." It was a matter of an infinite offense demanding an infinite reparation. There was a *debt* to pay, mankind's. No one but Christ could pay it. There was no genial gift exchange: His death for our redemption. And because the sacrifice of the Mass is the same sacrifice as that of the cross, it too falls into the category of debt-payment. Though it is an unbloody sacrifice, it is a real and true sacrifice, the payment of Jesus' life in a mystic way.

The Mass pays mankind's debts which otherwise would

never be cleared up. But sometimes books on the Mass deal with its aspect as gift: we offer a gift (bread and wine) to God and receive back His gift, Christ. This is a beautiful thought, but is it secondary? The fundamental idea back of the Mass is that it is a *debt paid to God*. It is something we owe in justice, something we've got to pay. God is offended by our sins; how are we to patch things up with our dearest Friend? An adequate plea for forgiveness is needed. The Mass.

On God's side, the Mass is not simply His giving us a gift. It is first and foremost His giving us something we cannot get along without, something we must have to live healthy Catholic lives. A mother doesn't call her children in to a piping hot meal with the words, "Here is a gift for you." She would be a strange mother if she did. For the dinner is something the children's bodies demand, that they can't do without.

Does the concept of gift help us see the Mass in its primary role as the discharge of an obligation to God? Or does it obscure this fundamental notion of the Mass? Does it tend to present the Mass as an item we can take or leave alone? As something we are at liberty to use in worship, if we feel inclined? We think it does obscure the Mass's true role and perhaps gives a false impression of the necessity of the Mass.

Yet, there is a very good reason for looking at the Mass as a gift. First, the prayer *Te igitur* which starts the Canon. Here the priest begs God to accept "these gifts, these presents, these . . . sacrifices." "Gifts" is a translation of *dona*, "presents" of *munera*. But these Latin words have other meanings. *Dona* means also and especially "repayment." It comes from the verb *dono* which means not only "to give" but especially "to remit a debt or obligation." *Munera*, translated "presents," is often translated as office, duty, function, obligation. It is most frequently used to mean duty or obligation.

When we think of a gift or present, we may think in particular of a birthday present. It is something we need not give, but give freely. In fact, the idea of the gift-giver's being obligated to give destroys the whole notion of gift. St. Thomas claims that the concept of gift "contains the idea of a gratuitous giving."[1] When we give a gift, we have no obligation to give. It is just a nice gesture on our part. But when we pay our rent, we are not doing the landlord a favor. We are fulfilling an obligation.

What about the Mass? Is it an unnecessary favor or a necessary function? A payment or a present? A matter of inclination or of obligation? There are four goals or purposes of the Mass: (1) adoration, (2) thanksgiving, (3) reparation, (4) petition. Which of these is a matter of choice? Or are all necessary? Are any of them not required, so that when we do them we are doing something gratuitously? Which one could we exempt ourselves from?

In examining the four goals of the Mass, we can see for ourselves whether the Mass is mainly a donation or a debt-payment. Is the Mass satisfied, a propos these four goals, by the concept of gift?

1. ADORATION

The essence of religion is adoration of God. Religion isn't primarily concerned with our neighbor, except with reference to God. Good works that we do for our neighbor, though not the main concern of religion, can be fitted into it if they are done for God's sake. Then only are they something pertaining to religion. Religion essentially has God as object and interest,

---

[1] *Summa Theologica*, I, Question 38, Article 2, body of the article as translated by Anton Pegis in *Basic Writings of St. Thomas Aquinas* (New York: Random House, 1944), Vol. I, p. 361.

not neighbor. This is why a church is different from a welfare agency office or youth club. One little boy stopped going to his social-minded evangelical church on Sundays. A fellow parishioner gently asked him why he missed. "I'm tired of cookouts," he replied wearily.

The Mass, then, is at the very heart of religion because it is the perfect (and only perfect) way of adoring God. This fact is sometimes overlooked in our good-works-conscious society. "Religion," warned a sociologist and theologian in West Baden, Indiana, "is not to be identified with programs to help the poor, alcoholics, convicts, the sick. Surely it involves all these programs, but secondarily, and with reference to God."

Protestantism is responsible in large part for this emphasis on the good-works aspect of religion. It began by emphasizing faith, to the exclusion of good works, but has veered abruptly away from faith alone and today focuses itself largely on good works done for the neighbor. Why? Perhaps to avoid the hopelessness issuing from a belief that man's nature is rotten to the core. Bury that realization, then, of one's inner depravity under a plethora of good works. The Council of Trent (Denz. 835) condemned this Protestant fallacy, but that was not enough to halt the hegira of heresy farther and farther into religious Marxianism where truth and error mingle on an equal basis in abject egalitarianism of indifference.

Protestants were quickly cut off from the Mass and most of the sacraments, the chief instruments of divine grace. Some tried to solace themselves by asserting (for the first time) that everyone had grace in the same degree. Again that leveling process. Perhaps there was in the conscience of non-Catholic Christendom a realization that without the Mass they could not worship God adequately. Hence the concentration on *doing* — philanthropy, economic programs, welfare, and the rest. Such a focus of concentration is not bad, but it is no substitute for the divine Mass and sacraments.

We live in a Protestant milieu, and it may be in some cases that the Mass and sacraments have not yet come into their own as the foremost means of practicing the virtue of religion. (Americans, in general, may be more faithful than any peoples in their love and use of the Mass.) Hence, Mrs. Jones, sitting quietly and calmly in church one morning hearing Mass, may be disturbed by the temptation that she is not helping her neighbor as much as if she were out distributing packages of food or soliciting funds for a new wing of the local hospital.

The truth is that at Mass Mrs. Jones is fulfilling a primary and inalienable obligation to God in the best possible way. Though it cannot be perceived by the senses, it is nonetheless true. "Even though something is not evident to the senses," wrote a student of the liturgy, "it can still be important, meritorious, profitable, worth doing, better than a lot of hectic physical activity. So when 'participation' is spoken of with regard to the Mass, it is equivalent in many minds with physical movement or propulsion or portage, such as processions, carrying candles, tapers, lecterns, veils, bells. 'Taking part in the Mass' is never referred to when a man is just sitting there *using his will* to love, adore, and worship God. The physical activities are important, even necessary for some (like the priest and servers). But 'participation' must not be *identified* with this motion, with prostrations, washings of feet or fingers, reading or turning pages, lighting tapers or blowing them out, or kissing something, however good these may be."

There is a vital point there: it is the will, the soul's activity, which enables humans to "participate." When a man and woman exchange wedding vows, there is no exterior tumult to indicate a change has taken place. Their mere audible words are not sufficient, in fact, to make their marriage contract valid. Something else is required, the act of the will. That is the essential thing!

The change in bread and wine producing the Eucharist occurs without any movement on the part of the bread and wine. The change is effected by the priest's will and softly spoken words. So too the Incarnation. At the *fiat*, the mere will act, of Mary, mankind's history swung from its downward plunge and began a rocket-like ascent to its greatest dignity. What of the man incurably sick? Christ said, "I *will*, be thou made clean."

There are many changes which occur without fanfare, hullabaloo, or noise but which are mighty changes. At the consecration of bread and wine there are no thunderclaps, no blinding flashes of lightning, no crash of thunder. There are no shrieks or moans, no shrill cries of triumph, nor cannon roaring. Reverent silence accompanies this mighty change. Like the silent change of the dead white of winter to the fresh, moist green that covers the world in spring. Like the change that transforms the frozen, still countenance of a winter stream into a leaping, dancing rivulet alive with rippling laughter.

Most of the important changes in our lives are silent and mysterious. Baptism bound us to Christ in some silent baptistery while the world went on as before, never knowing that in the stillness God had drawn to His heart a new adopted son. The sinner kneeling in the darkened confessional breathes his act of contrition while the confessor quietly pronounces the words of absolution. The forgiveness of sins, according to all the saints, is a greater miracle than creation. Yet what silence!

The atom and hydrogen bombs lead us to identify gigantic, earth-battering explosions and towering clouds of smoke and debris with power and importance. But nuclear fission releases only *one* kind of energy, and it is not the most important kind. The Mass releases another, divine energy which operates in the soul most powerfully. To the timorous, fearful, nescient Apostles the Holy Ghost came like a roaring wind and blazing points of fire. To modern Christians He comes like the gently whispering zephyr, yet no less effectively.

Hearing Mass is our "chief duty"[2] without all the physical commotion. Physical activity is not and has never been the measure of our devotion to God. Good works merit a reward only if they issue from the love of God. First comes love, then the good works, as external outshinings of the interior love.

We cannot escape the duty to make recognition of God's supremacy (adoration). A child cannot cancel out his obligations to his parents, or alter the fact he is their child. Man is God's child, creature of His limning. There is no escaping that truth. Worship is acknowledging it, often in a formal, public fashion. Religion is the means by which this acknowledgment is made, and in religion the sacrifice of the Mass functions officially in that role. Christ instituted it for that purpose: to pay God the recognition that His being what He is demands. No other way (than the Mass) will satisfy.

In discussing adoration there is no room for a concept of the Mass as a free gift. We must have the Mass to adore perfectly, and those who were without the Mass adored imperfectly. The merits of Calvary in anticipated fashion helped souls long before Annas and Caiphas and their gang were realities on the Jerusalem scene. In a sense, the application of those merits to souls before the Cross is a kind of anticipation of the Mass.

Even Sinanthropus pekinensis, in his bed of Chou Kou Tien

---

[2] *Mediator Dei*, Vatican Library translation (Washington, D. C.: National Catholic Welfare Conference), No. 80.

west of Peking, worshiped God and perhaps saved his soul by virtue of Masses one day to be offered, whether he knew it or not. All mankind is bound into one by the common (and uncommon) love of Christ coming from His Father and made over to all who love Jesus.[3] All men of good will are united in the common love of Christ for His Father; all are also united in the common worship paid God by Jesus in the Mass. It is *our* (meaning humanity's) way to worship God. The Mass cannot be locked away into the hour and place of its being offered, but reaches out everywhere (except into hell) with its boundless measure of hope and consolation.

The *timelessness* of the efficacy of the Mass is interesting and consoling. Yet it is a greater consolation to consider the *timeliness* of the Mass. For the Mass helps us here and now in *this* need, spiritual or temporal. One priest remarked, "I was strongly tempted to give up my studies for the priesthood every summer vacation. Only daily Mass saved me. I owe to it all that I have."

The Mass (1) gives us graces here and now, and (2) stores up spiritual power for the future. There will be times when we will need special help. The Masses we attend now put that strength toward our account, something for us to draw on. We will have that power "in reserve." Young Tom Sherwood, only 27, went to Mass as often as he could in Catholic-hating sixteenth-century England. On February 7, 1577, an official of the English courts told the young man that he was going to be hanged, drawn, and quartered. "Lord Jesus," he replied, "I am not worthy to suffer this for You, much less to receive those rewards You promised to those who love You." He was a martyr for the Mass, thanks to the graces stored away for him to use in time of crisis.

---

[3] Cf. Jn. 17:26.

The Mass, like its Founder, is always the same in its essence — in every clime and every time. Our moods and muddles, chameleon-like, eddy in perpetual change; but the Mass is changeless. It offers, day in day out, perfect and infinite love, devotion, and service to God on behalf of humans, *all humans.* King St. Louis IX of France went to daily Mass, no matter how pressing the duties of state might have been. The peasant girl Alpais assisted calmly and attentively at Mass every day from her little room off the church. She became the "saint of the Eucharist" (all saints of the New Testament are really saints of the Eucharist). Alpais is the earliest mystic of whom it is reliably recorded that she lived for years on nothing but the Blessed Sacrament.

There is joy and resounding optimism in the Mass.

2. THANKSGIVING

In the prayer after receiving the Host in Mass, the priest is directed to say, "What shall I give the Lord in return for all He has given to me?" (*Quid retribuam Domino pro omnibus quae retribuit mihi?*) And then he answers his own question by receiving another time the Same One that he is trying to "repay" God for! "Calicem salutaris accipiam. . . ." To repay God for one, no, for *all* the benefits, he will take the same Benefit again. To thank God for such a gift as the Eucharist, he will receive that same gift again! What an interesting thing! We can thank God for His benefits by accepting more benefits, *the* Benefit! Oh, but we recall that the Eucharist is the "Thank-Sacrament," so why not thank God by means of the sacrament specially fitted and made up for that purpose: The "Thank-Sacrament"? That is what the word *eucharist* means: to show thanks (*eu + charizesthai*).

19

The Eucharist is something altogether special — special in many ways. It is, for instance, the only sacrament a person can give to himself. All the others need someone else to administer them. We cannot baptize or confirm or shrive ourselves. But we can give ourselves Holy Communion. In Mexico during the persecutions not so many years ago the people had permission to give themselves Communion. And even outside persecution, it can be done. On the missions, where there is often occasion for the priest to be absent from the mission station, scholastics and brothers regularly have permission to give themselves Communion.

Is this an indication that Holy Communion is altogether special? Or shall we say, *another* indication that it is altogether special? For special it surely is! No greater intimacy can there be on earth with God: in my soul and in my body, Body and Blood, Soul and eternal divinity, Father, Son, and Holy Ghost in me! Small wonder that the Eucharist also "thanks" God for us.

In the Mass of the Chaldean Liturgy, while the celebrant is preparing bread and wine at the altar, the people chant a hymn of thanks to God called the *Lakhumara*. The ritual of our whole life should be accompanied by its own *Lakhumara*, hymn of thanks. Children are taught early to say "Thank you" for a favor, even the slightest. We thank friends for favors, and we even thank others for doing their duty: policemen for directing us to our destination, store clerks for selling us merchandise. This is a good practice. No one loves an ingrate.

Do we thank God for His gifts? Do we, can we, aptly tell Him we are grateful? Our debt of thanks depends on the equality of gift and giver. God's gifts are natural possessions, life, health, opportunities, talents, His precious graces He died on the cross to merit for us, faith, the whole complexus of our religion. And He, an infinite Person, gave them. How can we ease this burden of indebtedness?

Sometimes, the greatest gift of all leaves us speechless. Speechlessness is one of our ways of showing gratitude. Perhaps this helps explain the profound silence of the Canon of the Mass. The Mass is the unique, the perfect way of saying "Thanks." The entire Preface is a *Lakhumara* of its own. "It is fitting and just that we should thank you, holy Lord. . . ."

We must thank God. "It is fitting and just" to say "Thanks," says the Preface. We are bound in justice to give thanks. There is no choice. God expects us to be grateful, and to tell Him so. He knows our hearts, but He wants to hear the song of our lips. "Were not all ten made clean?" He asked sadly of the lepers He had cured. "And the other nine, where are they? Not one has come back to give God the praise except this stranger" (Lk. 17:17, 18). The Mass alone pays our debt of gratitude. Without it we are tongue-tied. No question of a gift here. We are dealing with a debt, something due.

We have to work at developing a *sense of gratitude*. Although it is natural, yet it can be so long submerged by the busy life of today that it is lost sight of. We have to salvage it. Reading, thinking about it, *practicing* gratitude and thanksgiving will do that salvage job. One housewife remarked of how she almost lost her sense of gratitude. "I longed for the day when we would have a house with enough bedrooms for the children. Then one day we had that house. There were five bedrooms. But all of a sudden I found myself not thinking of how lucky we were to have the big house and the five bedrooms but grousing about the terrific job of landscaping the place, complaining about the dust, and thinking of what an absolutely endless job of work lay ahead. I snapped out of that in a hurry. Whenever I feel blue at the dust or at the slowness of the lawn in coming up, I just think of those five fine bedrooms."

A sense of gratitude doesn't just materialize: it must be produced by persistent effort. When Andrew Carnegie, the steel king, wanted to pay his thanks to Charles Schwab, he paid him a salary of $1 million per year. When we want to pay our thanks to God, we have something worth more than any sum of money: the Mass. And it returns our thanks in the best possible way. For in the Mass, the one who says "Thanks" for us is Jesus Christ.

3. REPARATION

"Sin, so far as it is possible to it, destroys God." That is St. Bernard's graphic pen-picture of the effects of the world's worst evil — and only true evil. Yet we are callous. "It is an old tale, now," gloomed the prophet Jeremias, "how thou didst break in pieces the yoke of my dominion, didst sever all the bonds between us, crying out, I will serve no more!" (2:20.) What magic words can resurrect our awareness of sin and its profoundly evil nature?

Sin is the reverse of grace. Grace taps the power of God at its source for the strength to believe in, love, and serve God as He deserves. The soul with grace is not replaced by God or by some quality of God, but is brought into closest union with Him. "Your life is hidden away now with Christ in God" was how St. Paul put it (Col. 3:3). Our mind and will draw off from the riches of God a dynamic power which lifts them to a new plane of activity.

Sin wrecks all this.

In sinning we throw overboard God's love and help — Himself. For what? For a commotion of the glands, a few shadowy years of power and luxury, for unease and restlessness here — and hell hereafter.

Is there any way of mending the fences knocked down in our unreasoning haste to sin? If there is some adequate purification, it must be more than human. It was a magnificent gesture in which God made us His children; sin spurns this generosity. It is the son's disobedience that hurts most, not the hired man's. We must make up with God. Even in purely human affairs, God asks us to patch up our quarrels before offering our gift at the altar. All the more must we repair for sin.

Recently in Boston a panel of distinguished men, among them two priests, discussed guilt. Why does it gnaw at men's souls? Why is it so common? The Catholic answer, in general, is that it is not much more common than sin which often produces it. Smashing the indescribably beautiful edifice of grace with its relationships of intimacy with God, has deep-rooted effects on a man. If he feels guilty, it is because he *is* guilty. Purification involves sorrow, confession — and the Mass.

The Mass drives us toward unpleasant contrition, so ill-fitting to our misshapen human pride. But it does more than that. It pays the temporal debt of punishment due to our sin. It reconstructs the harmony and equilibrium between God and man that sin knocked into discordant jangle. No question here of gift, but of debt, obligation.

For mankind hounded by guilt and guilt complexes, the Mass is a must. We might, in a sense, say that in the Mass we bring a "gift" to God. But immediately we have to add that it is such a gift that the world could not get along without giving! Our intelligent participation in the Mass is the heart of our purification. Contact with God in the Mass is what puts our nature right with itself and God. Sometimes other things are put forward as panaceas for the malaise of modern man — whatever that is. Some say we are out of tune with Nature (with a capital N). Purification will come from our meeting with seasons and soil, some sort of divorce from machinery is necessary or implied. There is, say these writers, a relationship between our spiritual advancement and our being in tune with Nature. Not atonement but attunement is at the root of purification for them.

The attitude that any type of work but cultivating the soil is "artificial" goes against the deepest considerations of man's capabilities. His primary capabilities are for intellectual and artistic operations. Man is least capable when it comes to digging in the soil. Compared to the gopher, the fire ant, and the mole, man's body is poorly equipped for moving mountains of soil. But when he is using his intellect, his reason, his imagination, his controlled emotions, he is then a supreme performer because he is doing what is natural to him as a human.

Some spiritual writers exaggerate the importance of "contact with the seasons and the soil" in forming a soul that is receptive to contemplation of divine truth. They may even regard as artificial anything produced for man's life or betterment by machines. This is a mistake. It is as natural for man to produce machines as it is for gophers to burrow in the ground. "Artificial" can connote many things. It sometimes indicates a certain dislocation of man from his environment, as though man did not belong rightfully to that kind of environment.

The most natural thing to man is to make artifacts, because artifacts are things constructed by means of his human intelligence. It is natural for man to use his imagination to create artificial supplements to his bodily and intellectual powers. The electronic brain is supremely natural to man because it is so excellent a supplement to his intellectuality.

The native of Tanganyika crouching in terror during an electrical storm is not acting as naturally (according to his entire complement of natural powers) as the man who has protected himself by lightning rods.

"Artificial" is not a bad thing. And to say that our life is artificial is complimentary rather than dyslogistic or uncomplimentary. Sometimes the Mass is said to be "artificial." But whether it is said in the morning or evening, at high noon or Christmas midnight, is of no great significance. The saving of souls is timeless. Sanctification is an echo of eternity. The liturgical functions may borrow elements from the seasonal cycle, but that is secondary to their central significance, namely, sanctification.

When the terms "natural" and "artificial" are contrasted, people usually think that "natural" is better. Is it? Artificial light has saved many lives (and eyes). The crude surgical methods once employed and the primitive concoctions of herbs may be closer to nature than mechanical hearts and lungs and carefully manufactured anesthetics. But they are not better. Nor as good, in fact, not near.

The Mass is in many respects "artificial." But this enhances it. The ritual, the rhetorical elements of the prayers, even the movements of its ministers are artificial to a great extent. Hence, we are not surprised that instruction concerning the meaning of the Mass is necessary. This we should recognize as normal. I have heard people say how incongruous it is to have to explain the Mass which should itself be an explanation. But such explanation is natural when we are dealing with artificial things, and a constant need among succeeding generations of maturing Catholics.

Just because something grows out of the soil does not mean it is better than something which required exceptional technical knowledge and special manufacture. Sassafras tea is a mild diaphoretic. But when little Andrea Crossland of Omaha, born with a hole in her heart, underwent remedial surgery successfully, it required highly artificial techniques to save her life. The surgeon had to instruct his assistants and teach them the minute details of this elaborate operation. When she came out of the anesthetic, 9-year-old Andrea's first words were, "Where is the priest? I must get to Communion every day." Exceedingly artificial techniques saved Andrea, not some "natural" antidotes of vintage medicine men.

The natural and spontaneous prayer may be very good but it is not as good and effective as the elaborately artificial liturgy which we call the Mass. The Mass saves lives, too; because of its artificiality, it too requires explanation to those who would use and appreciate it. This is not surprising.

4. PETITION

What was the most significant event of the past century? The discovery of atomic fission? The establishment of the United Nations? The rise of Communism? The growth of the prestige of the Papacy? Each of these factors has shaped history and influenced the lives of millions. But none is of chief moment. The offering of a single Mass outranks them all. The shadow of the cross falls upon all of history, giving it form and meaning; the Mass contains and is the sacrifice of the cross.

Such a consideration is especially important when we consider the stepchild of the four goals of the Mass, petition, the "gimme" part of all our prayer. It is imperative; Christ demands it of us. "Ask . . . seek . . . knock . . ." not once but repeatedly, insistently. Asking comes naturally to the Christian; he is not ashamed to ask, to beg. His Father wants him to do just that. The habit of asking helps a man realize just how inadequate he is on his own hook. Christianity is not a "do-it-yourself" religion; it is a co-operative venture, God and man united in Christ. And always the first move, the first spark of love, the first impulse of sorrow, must come from God. He will unfailingly give us this spark; we need only ask. In the Mass, Christ asks with and for us. Blessed Claude la Colombière once wrote: "However vast my desires may be, however great my hopes, I make no difficulty in asking all that can satisfy them. . . . I even believe that I do wrong to this living Victim by asking infinitely less than It is worth!"

By another divine paradox, we find that one of God's gifts (the Mass) is the perfect means by which we thank Him for *all* His gifts. This realization prompted Blessed Claude to say, "I shall say Mass every day. That is my only resource."

A housewife and mother of five once observed that the difficulties in her life often distracted her at Mass. "I feel that my perplexity over them," she said, "is taking away from the value of my worship at Mass." In fact, those very perplexities are just what we should bring to Mass. Blessed Rose Philippine Duchesne came from France in 1818 to help establish the Religious of the Sacred Heart in the United States and to teach Catholic doctrine, from New Orleans even to the Potawatomie Indians in Kansas. They used to call her *Quah-kah-ka-num-ad* ("Woman-Who-Prays-Always"). Whenever the Jesuit priests made their annual retreat in Florissant, Missouri, she stayed in the church for all their Masses, sometimes nine in a row, and only left when they were all finished. She got from the Mass calm strength, irrepressible courage, unfailing good humor. She unblushingly asked, again and again, at Mass after Mass, several each day whenever possible, for the graces she needed. Through these many Masses God blessed this extraordinary soul whose influence still works among the

27

American people. "Poor America!" she wrote in 1825 from Missouri. "When one thinks that between here and Canada and to the west as far as the Pacific Ocean there is not a single church, not one priest, it is just heartbreaking."[4] The enormous change in the condition of the Church in America in the intervening 36 years is due in no small way to this gray-headed, toothless, dear, and courageous soul whom some who knew her called "poor devil," because of her un-prepossessing exterior. Thus does the Mass, God's own devotion, the devotion of the universal Church in all ages and all climes, answer the deep-felt needs of all God's children.

Just how adequately does the concept of Mass as our "gift" to God correspond to this absolute necessity of asking, begging, importuning God? Since the Mass is the only adequate means we have of making our requests for supernatural benefits of immeasurable worth, "gift" must give way to "debt-payment" once again. Pius XII put it this way: "God himself wishes that there should be a continuation of this sacrifice [of Calvary] . . . so that there may be no cessation of the hymn of praise and thanksgiving which man *owes* to God, seeing that he *requires* God's help continually and he has *need* of the blood of the Redeemer to remit sin which challenges God's justice."[5] There we have it: the four aims of the Mass — to adore, to thank, to make reparation, to ask. And in each case, the Holy Father uses words, "owes," "requires," "need," which can be applied only awkwardly to a "gift." We must give God adoration, praise, thanks, reparation. Thanks to the Mass, we can perfectly fulfill these obligations with richest rewards for ourselves.

"I don't like the idea of praying to God only for what I can get out of Him," a devout lawyer told me. Yet it was this

---

4 *Philippine Duchesne* by Louise Callan, Newman Press, 1957, p. 430.
5 *Mediator Dei*, NCWC translation, 79.

same God who encouraged us to come to Him to get refreshment, food, and drink for our thirsting souls, peace of heart. "Utilitarianism" is a word we often use in a derogatory sense, because we may fail to observe that if something is valuable, it must for that reason be *useful*. Even the word "useful" has fallen into some disrepute. This is unfortunate because we may tend to disparage what is useful and to prefer in its stead the merely beautiful, the merely aesthetic. Most of the items we find in museums have a value, though many of them are relatively useless; but we can hardly value enough the useful things the Church provides for our use. Pre-eminent among these is the Mass. To some it seems unworthy to value the Mass for its usefulness to man. They place its value in other, even sentimental, attachments. The proclivity we may sometimes feel for preferring what we are sentimentally attached to, rather than what is *merely* useful, is somewhat common. It enters even such a mundane field as stocks and bonds. A prominent investment counseling company in the East lists just such a romantic tendency as a major reason for many poor investments. Instead of purchasing stocks and bonds which are tailored to their income and general financial position, some investors buy unsuitable stocks because "the wife has a sentimental attachment to them," or because "Mother always bought them," or simply out of habit.

Now the Mass is the most useful thing we possess. Since God Himself attached this usefulness to the Mass, He expects us to value the Mass for this quality and to use it to help ourselves and others. Its value does not lie in sentimental attachments. Precisely this is pointed out in the altar boy's response to the priest's injunction after the Offertory, "Orate fratres," Pray brethren. The server, in the name of all the people, replies, "May the Lord accept the sacrifice from your hands for the praise and glory of His own name, for our *utility* (*utilitatem*) and for the *utility* of the entire holy Church."

The king of France remarked one day to Henry I of England (1100–1135) that a person ought to miss Mass occasionally in order to hear a sermon. Henry replied that it was a greater pleasure to him to see his Friend (Christ) than to hear someone else praise Him. Obviously Henry recognized the utility of the Mass, for he usually heard three Masses every day from his special place on the altar steps (the royal prerogative), sometimes even placing his hand under the priest's arm during the elevation of the Body and Blood of Christ. Henry has been described as systematic, hard-headed, with a legal bent of mind and a passion for justice and order. Perhaps these traits helped him to realize how perfectly the Mass satisfies the profound needs of human nature, and to *use* it accordingly. So should we.

Your Peace of Mind

In 1957 the Japanese people spent $3.5 million for a tranquilizing drug called meprobamate. Time was when other means supplied for humans that precious self-control which makes tranki (as the Japanese call the "worry-killing" pills) superfluous. One of these means was the tea ceremony imported from China. Said a veteran missiologist, "That is the pattern of the Orient: control the outside first, and hope that the inside will eventually conform itself."

Peace of mind is obviously high on the list of most-wanted items on everybody's shopping list. We need not be tea drinkers to win it. Indication of interest in peace of mind, Father John C. Ford, S.J., has remarked, is the clutch of popular jokes centering on the psychoanalyst's couch. Psycho-analysis is one means of gaining mental balance. Tranquilizers may also help, have in fact enthusiastically been said to herald "a new era in the management of the mentally disturbed patient."[1]

Peace is what human beings were promised, not when tea or drugs or couches were announced, but when the Son of God was ushered into the world. He is the divine analgesic to soothe disturbed hearts. And He chooses to administer the curative of Himself in the sacrifice of the Mass.

The Mass is the answer to man's need for peace of mind. It promises and delivers it. The word *peace* (with derivatives) occurs 11 times in the Mass of the Latin Rite, 29 times in the Liturgy of the Copts, 28 times in the Byzantine Liturgy, 26 times in the Liturgy of Malabar. Like a refrain, the word *peace* relentlessly repeats, pouring from hearts in need of true peace. Peace of mind is the only true peace — not as Livy says of the Romans: "Solitudinem faciunt, pacem appellant." (They make a desert and call it peace, i.e., by killing off all the people and laying waste the land!) No, that was the Roman idea of peace. True peace is in the soul; it is found, not by destroying others but by conquering oneself.

Cell 23 in Neveu Prison, Shanghai, was only 20 by 15 feet, but it cooped up 15 political prisoners. One of them was a 22-year veteran of the Chinese mission. French Jesuit Father André Bonnichon kept a memory-log of his ten months' mind scrubbing by the Red brain-washermen. Extended quizzing un-der blinding floodlights, a daily six-hour examination of con-science to discover sins against the Red Chinese government, loudspeakers decibellowing the sins they were expected to find —

---

[1] Wyeth Laboratories of Philadelphia used this phrase in describing their recent product, Sparine.

these were the techniques the "People's" government pioneered to pulverize the masses and knead them into a pliant dough. For exercise each day, the men in cell 23 walked in single-file round and round their pen, some staring stolidly at the ground, others exchanging furtive whispers. "I prefer keeping silence," recorded Father Bonnichon. "This matutinal merry-go-round within our four walls can be devoted to the Canon of the Mass in which I unite myself to the Masses that are being said all over the world."

Peace of mind was no stock in trade in this dim, flea-bitten stronghold of tyranny, cell 23. The prisoners were forbidden to hold their heads up or stand when their cell door was opened. Gradually they lost their self-respect and their sanity, confessed "crimes" of their reactionary past just to be set free. They even began to believe the lies about themselves their Communist captors daily dinned into their ears. Yet Father Bonnichon salvaged his peace of mind.

My companions [he wrote], earth-bound creatures, are indeed imprisoned. It's their boast that they are, one and all, clods of animated matter, and that this cell of ours confines every atom of their being. I'm the lucky one! All I need is the spiritual leap by which I present myself before my Heavenly Father, whose eye is on me day and night. . . . My relegation to this cell here and my captivity (with its hint of the night of the Passion) far from expressing separation feeds this profound and consoling sense of union. Could anything be more futile than the mechanical gyration of these men around me, shut out as they are from faith and hope? For me, in contrast, every round takes me round the world, in the Sacrifice of the Church for the benefit of the Church (*pro Ecclesia Catholica*), offered on countless altars, for "the salvation of the whole world." Each of my footsteps on this wooden floor leaves its impress on eternity.[2]

---

[2] Father Bonnichon's article, translated by Father L. E. Bellanti, appeared in the Jan. and Feb. issues of *Month*, 1955. The quotations here are from the January issue, p. 13. The series was entitled "Cell 23 . . . Shanghai."

From 1931, when at the age of 29 the Jesuit arrived in China, missionary cross newly gleaming, till June 15, 1953, when he was arrested in his office at Aurora University, his life had been lived for others. Then came imprisonment, the missionary's crucifixion. On April 22, 1954, the former dean of the law faculty at Aurora University was expelled from China. In what curious cranny of cell 23 did he find what millions of comfort-cosseted humans in the free world are searching so frenetically for: peace of mind? The answer is: he found peace of mind in the holy Mass.

Peace of mind can be had only if we face reality. "Lord, that I may see," the blind man begged Christ. That plea is made anew and granted in the Mass: the sight of things, of our own defects and needs, as they really are. How many millions are grasping for peace, and failing to reach it! Every year 310,000 people commit suicide, according to statistician Louis Dublin. Most of them are in far better circumstances than the Jesuit missionary, than the average citizen. What had he, and thousands of other well-balanced, well-adjusted individuals that the suicides, neurotics, alcoholics, and worry warts do not have?

One thing the latter have is a sense of insecurity, common root of unhappiness. The solution is to develop a consciousness of one's own personal value. The Mass above all inculcates such a consciousness. First: by actually increasing the individual's value, giving him a greater share of divine grace, measure of worth in the eyes of God. Second: by making him more and more aware of the value of grace, of God's love of the soul. "We solemnize the day," reads the third prayer of the Canon on Holy Thursday, "on which our Lord Jesus Christ was delivered up *for us.*" We are the reason for His sufferings and death. In the Creed of the Council of Nicea (A.D. 325), the Fathers of the Church wrote that God became man "for

34

us and for our salvation." That profound expression of the value of every single human is reiterated in every Sunday Mass: *Credo in unum Deum.*

The Mass helps us to face reality. Man has a tendency to avoid unpleasant situations — a "negative psychotaxis" psychologists call it. The man who was sacked gets drunk, the bankrupt gulps half a bottle of sleeping pills, the jilted woman suddenly loses her ability to speak (*aphonia*). Some flee so far from reality that they lose touch with it completely, viz., the manic depressive, the schizophrenic. They live in a mental world of their own making.

But no problem was ever solved by flight. What is needed is the "truth-giving spirit" promised by Christ to the Twelve, and by the Church to those at Mass.[3] The Gospel of the day always contains a special message. In the Liturgy (Mass) of the Armenians, just before the deacon chants the Gospel he says in Greek, "Be attentive!" And the celebrant rejoins, "It is God who speaks." Father Agostino Bea, S.J., confessor to Pius XII and noted Scripture scholar, has urged Bible reading at Mass. "The most adequate place for the Word of God," he has declared, "is the Mass where it predisposes the soul for the reception of Communion. Christ in the Last Supper united the Gospel and the Sacrifice of the Eucharist."

Facing up to our needs won't crush us. Regardless of our deficiencies, we cannot be engulfed in the faceless welter of humanity. The human soul is far too precious for that. Most of us are "haunted by a feeling of inadequacy," according to Father Conleth Overman, C.P., who has had great experience in counseling souls. "This is especially true if one has any ideals in the field in which he works." More than feelings of inadequacy plague us. Most authorities believe that one third

---

[3] Jn. 14:16, 17, Gospel of Mass on Eve of Pentecost.

of our population is damaged in work, health, and happiness by neuroses. That would be more than 50 million humans, in the U. S. alone, agitated by worry, guilt complexes, phobias, frustration, and insecurity!

What is the Gospel answer? "Joy to you in the Lord at all times; once again I wish you joy . . . may the peace of God, which surpasses all our thinking, watch over your hearts and minds in Christ Jesus."[4] Joy implies mastery of emotions. "A person has reached emotional maturity," according to the noted psychologist, Father Raphael McCarthy, S.J., "when he has developed the ability to manage his own emotional responses." The mature man isn't thrown out of joint by small (or large) problems, not flung into deep gloom by setbacks or trials. He can handle the situations of each day without losing peace of mind. The Mass supplies us with (1) grace to be calm, (2) insight of ways to solve difficulties, (3) incentive of models, our Lord, the Blessed Mother, and the saints, presented to us in the liturgy.

In her book *Wake Up and Live,* Dorothea Brande remarks that a factor that paralyzes human industry and derails the most fervent crusader is "the will to fail." This invidious psychological down-in-the-mouthism may destroy as much as 80 per cent of our efficiency. After we carefully shape our goal, nourish our ambitions, and prepare ourselves for the struggle to reach the noble goal, we give up when the going gets rough. The Prince of Apostles, Peter himself, appears to have been a victim for a time of the "will to fail." Matthew, describing the scenes of the Passion of Jesus, says that "Peter followed (Christ) at a long distance, as far as the high priest's palace, where he went in . . . *to see the end*" (26:58). No hope there.

---

[4] Phil. 4:4, 7, epistle of the Mass on the Feast of St. John Bosco, January 31.

Advises author Brande: "Act as if it were impossible to fail."
If we unite with Christ in the Mass, it *is* impossible to fail
in the only area where true failure is found: the moral order.

Such an affirmative, optimistic, bright outlook on life guided
the famous Bishop Richard of Chichester. He was born about
1200, three years after a Worcestershire priest named Layamon
had penned his famous poem, *The Brut. The Brut* tells the
story of an English king named Leir. He had divided his kingdom between two daughters who had fulsomely flattered him.
The third daughter he disinherited because she had said simply
that she loved him as a daughter should love her father. The
poem is prophetic of what Richard's future had in store. He
was no more a flatterer of vain, lavish, pliable King Henry III
of England, than Cordoille was of Leir. And Richard, like
Cordoille, got exile for his honesty. Henry wanted yes-men.
The English nobles were angry with him because foreign
favorites were swarming into their land and hiving on the
choicest governmental offices. Richard's complaint was with
the monarch's attempts to select bishops. His blunt candor in
the matter did not endear him to the king.

Richard's peace of mind and unshakable calmness are the
more remarkable in view of his tempestuous career. As chancellor of the diocese of Canterbury under Archbishop Edmund,
Richard earned the king's disfavor for stanchly opposing the
royal bid to rule the Church. The king played his ace by
deporting both the archbishop and his chancellor as "unde-
sirables." Richard was permitted to return, as parish priest in
Deal, after Edmund had died. Later Rome appointed him
to the Bishopric of Chichester. King Henry had other ideas.
His nominee was a felon named Robert Passelewe, who had
coughed several thousand tainted marks into the royal ex-
chequer. Richard had to be consecrated in Lyons, France,

37

and returned to a hostile diocese. For two years he lived with Simon of Tarriez, as a missionary prelate, in a running duel with revenue-ravenous Henry III. Only the threat of an excommunication (the medieval pope's ace of trumps) made Henry relent. Richard moved to the bishop's residence.

Bishop Richard kept his goal in view, and worked doggedly to reach it. When he died in 1253, he was still in the prelatial harness, preaching a crusade against the Saracens. He never heard of "the will to fail." He worked with his powers at full capacity, never permitting himself to go to seed in a lazy Indian summer of pessimism and self-pity. The Mass puts our goal constantly before us: service of Christ in our duties. It sharpens our view of the goal, and makes the ideal become a reality by giving us the power to persevere. The Mass makes a happy, dynamic character.

Epicurus, whose philosophy of life (misinterpreted) has made him go down in eponymity, fixed serenity of soul as the goal of existence. Man's aim, said this Samos-born ex-soldier, is pleasure, but not pleasure as orgiastic license, as many understand Epicureanism today. This pleasure is to be found rather in serenity (*ataraxia*) of soul. This Greek work *ataraxia* is the same word that was borrowed to describe the new tranquilizer drugs, ataraxics. The Christian would not imitate Epicurus, by making serenity of soul the *goal* of life; but he would establish it as a necessary *means* to acquiring heroic virtue. Christ cannot be served properly by a man filled with unquietude, impatience, and impulsiveness.

Peace of mind can subsist on a minimum of material benefits, like the pipe-stem ocotillo cactus, finding food and drink who knows where in the desert soil. The county clerk in Cripple Creek, Colorado, famous old mining town, survived an infamous death march out of Russia during World War II. Four thousand prisoners began the long, frozen trudge in the middle of Russian winter. Forty pulled through. "I saved my life and sanity," the county clerk recalls, "by saying over and over again the parts of the Mass I could remember. I saved my life by uniting myself with the Mass going on all over the world." Meanwhile, others in the ragged, stumbling columns went stark mad and were shot by their guards. Several of the guards went crazy, began spraying bullets into the ranks of the prisoners, and had to be mowed down by other half-crazy guards. "The Mass saved me," says the man from Cripple Creek with a grateful shake of his head.

Frank, businesslike admission of guilt is a part of peace of mind. Commented a Jesuit who worked with prisoners in Alcatraz: "It's a rare bird who'll admit he's guilty and wasn't framed or rail-roaded." In the *Confiteor* priest and people confess their inadequacy and guilt. In the *Oration* God's grace is asked. In the *Gloria* we acknowledge God's infinite capacity to help us. Haughty self-sufficiency is unreal and untrue.

"A consciousness of personal value," a midwest psychologist has remarked, "is one thing needed to make life worth living. If we feel we are of no value to anyone, then we will think of ourselves as unwanted and worthless. We must make ourselves of value to people. Then they will value us." Criminologists assert that many crimes are expressions of an individual's desire for recognition he never got as a child. Physical ugliness may often be partly responsible for this lack of recognition. Plastic surgery is in such cases a part of the therapy for reclaiming the criminal for society. Psychogenic blindness is considered by many psychologists as often a product of emotional insecurity because of a lack of affection and love in the home.[5]

---

[5] Sigmund Freud characteristically attributed hysterical blindness to a revolt of the ego against the use of the eyes for obtaining sexual pleasure.

The Mass builds up a sense of personal value. First, by making our person more valuable, increasing in our souls our sharing in the priceless supernatural life of God. The Mass performs spiritual plastic surgery, engrafting in our souls the theological virtues of faith, hope, and charity, straightening out crooked wills by redirecting them toward God, brightening and enlarging the eye of the mind so that it might see God and others in Him with greater speed and accuracy. "Lord, thou dost throw thy loving kindness around us like a shield," exults the Offertory of the Mass of SS. John and Paul (June 26).

A young Montana pastor remarked at a clerical conference that "the Mass is calculated to engender an awareness of God's protective custody in every trifling detail of our lives. The prayers of the Mass are pervaded by this consciousness of Christ's concern for souls. This is precisely why many experts in the liturgical movement are eager for Mass in the vernacular. As it is now, countless Catholics are missing the significance and wonderful doctrine contained in the prayers. If people realized that God *does* care, that He *is* interested in them, would there be so much anxiety and frustration among Catholics?"

The self-control, thoroughness, humility, perseverance, self-denial, honesty, orderliness, simplicity, purity, charity, and cheerfulness needed to frame a peaceful life are presented to us in the prayers of the Mass and in the example of Christ in the Gospels and of the saints. Here lies the heart of the prayer-therapy of the Mass. "Just to list the virtues," commented an ex-Navy chaplain, "is a big incentive to practice them." The Mass lists the virtues of a full Christian life. The virtues glitter from the passages of Scripture read in the Epistles and Gospels. Present in the Mass is the Son of God, and it is He who lends His divine power to the Holy Sacrifice. With this power a man can transform his life, converting the abstract idea of a virtue into a living pattern of action, developing to the full extent the supernatural virtues planted and invigorated by the Mass.

Reduced to its simplest formula, the Mass and peace of mind are related in this fashion: Grace = a sharing in God's life and nature. "The profoundest peace rules in God and the most untroubled happiness."[6] Because the Mass gives us abundant gifts of grace, it enables us to possess more of God's peace and happiness. In sharing in His nature, we share in His unshakable peace of mind.

The saints were happy people. And they loved the Mass. Men and women at the early Mass in the church at Riva di Chieri, Italy, watched in astonishment as a frail five-year-old prepared the altar for Mass. "How on earth will he ever lift the book?" But Dominic Savio managed by grace and by grit; serving Mass was his favorite task. Of this little boy, now canonized, St. John Bosco remarked, "His cheerfulness and vivacity made him a favorite with the boys, even those who had no great love of religion." A young Bavarian went to daily Mass as a boy, quietly hearing the Masses and gazing at the crucifix above the altar. "The crucifix is my book," he said. Conrad of Parzham later became a Capuchin laybrother (he was not considered talented enough to become a priest) and a canonized saint. He died in 1894 at the age of 76 and was canonized in 1934.

In 1917, in the midst of a great war popularly termed "the last," the patent Friedrich Bayer & Co. of Germany held on aspirin expired. Since then the consumption of aspirin has

---

[6] *The Mysteries of Christianity* by Matthias Scheeben, translated by Cyril Vollert, S.J. (St. Louis: B. Herder Book Co., 1946), p. 105.

increased at the rate of 10 per cent per year, and Monsanto Chemical Company, which began producing aspirin in 1917, has become the world's largest aspirin producer. Americans hopefully swallow 12 billion aspirin tablets (or 6000 tons of aspirin) every year! How many tons of Sacred Hosts are consumed? Wars begot anxiety, anxiety begot headaches, and headaches begot aspirin. For America's king-sized headache, 6000 tons of aspirin are produced each year. For a whole world's ills, God has bequeathed the Mass and Eucharist. They are our chief sources of peace of mind.

John Baptist de Rossi, sickly and hollow-eyed with a burning fever, clutched at a remedy for both soul and body, not in aspirin, but in the Mass. As a boy in Voltaggio, north of Genoa, he served as many Masses as he could after his first class in the morning. Later, as a secular priest (now canonized), he was dubbed *Venator Animarum*, Hunter after Souls. His soul was at peace with God and man though housed in a jerry-built body and besieged by activity.

An old Arkansas caretaker whose father had been a plantation slave used to say, "A watched pot neveh boils. Dat's true de pot uv happiness too. Search yo' life away fo' it, and you'll find nothin'. Turn yo' back on it and it'll get holt of you quickern a cornered coon." The brilliant Victorian philosopher and economist John Stuart Mill discovered the same thing: that the pot of happiness never boils over into our lives if we watch it. At 20 Mill lurched into a bog of futilitarian depression. It was 1826, midway through the "era of Metternich." Heinrich Heine was writing his most delightful lyric poems. But for Mill life was not lyric. Beethoven was a year from death. But Mill could find no beauty in music. He was rescued from the mire by a passage gleaned from the *Memoires* of Marmontel: "those only are happy who have their minds fixed on some object other than their own happiness; on the happiness of others, on the improvement of mankind, even on some art or pursuit followed not as a means, but itself as an ideal end. Aiming thus at something else they find happiness by the way." The old Arkansas caretaker in his hut beside the canebrake discovered the same thing in his pot of sow belly and black-eyed peas that never boiled while he sat and watched.

"I am here among you as your servant," said the Son of God to the bickering twelve. Like Christ, Christians are to serve others; there lies their happiness. The Mass is the principal means of assisting souls. "No other work," in the famous words of the Council of Trent, "can be performed by the faithful which is so holy and divine as this tremendous mystery (the Mass)" (Session 22). Hence, the life of the Christian will to a large extent be turned outward. Peace of mind eludes those who are self-centered. Altruism is the trademark of the saint. The question is: how altruistic, how devoid of thoughts of self, should our love of God and man be?

A Jesuit theologian from St. Mary's College, St. Marys, Kansas, replied: "Perhaps our love can be altogether forgetful of self, though this may be argued. The question might be: *should* it be? Can a human being's love become so simply disinterested that it has *no* regard for self? That such a thing should happen would seem to go against the very nature of man and his fundamental human capabilities. It could, of course, happen that a person would so forget himself that he would think *only* of the other fellow's welfare. But is that normal? Is that natural?"

And he added: "Is it not less perfect, in fact, to forget oneself entirely — since our whole aim and obligation in life is to save our own soul first? Wouldn't it be an abnormality

43

for a person so to forget himself that he became altogether engrossed in the other person's welfare? No less an abnormality than the opposite."

Both our "disinterested love" (called *amor benevolentiae* by theologians) and our "interested love" (or *amor concupiscentiae*) must exist side by side without priority. The great Scheeben held that these two types of love inevitably involve each other. Wrote he: "Love of friendship necessarily longs for union with God. . . . For whoever desires to possess God on account of His goodness, thereby desires to be taken up by that goodness and to be possessed."[7]

It is impossible to love and serve God without getting a reward. Why, then, refuse to think about the reward? Father Grandmaison has pointed out that Jesus centered the thoughts of His hearers on the thought of reward. So does the Mass. The Introit of the Mass on the Feast of St. Joseph the Workman (May 1) is a sample: "Wisdom has paid to those who are just the reward of their labors."

Our love of God and man necessarily involves our love of ourselves. So, the Mass, which renders for us the perfect adoration, thanks, and reparation to God, also and at the same time brings to us the greatest reward. There is no need to try to separate the love and the reward. We cannot love God without profiting. We cannot hear Mass without doing ourselves the greatest possible favor.

Suffering, if mishandled, upsets peace of mind. Where does the suffering come from? Mental suffering, Freud thought, stems from man's instinctual drives. Harry Stack Sullivan, founder of the Washington (D. C.) School of Psychiatry,

---

[7] *Nature and Grace* by Matthias Scheeben, translated by Cyril Vollert, S.J. (St. Louis: B. Herder Book Co., 1954), p. 245 ff., especially p. 270, from which the quotation is taken.

maintained that suffering stemmed from "poor relationship with other men." The most popular nonfiction work in America was written precisely to help men improve their relationships with others. *How to Win Friends and Influence People* by Dale Carnegie has sold more than four million copies. It lays siege to such vices as criticizing, thoughtlessness, wrangling, gloominess; exalts honest praise, cheerfulness, being a good listener, showing affability toward all.

The spiritual director of a small diocesan seminary in the southern United States pointed out that these are the very virtues that the Church requires of a candidate for canonization. In one popular life of St. Philip Neri, Father Filippo is cited as being outstanding in the very virtues Carnegie extolled in hotel ballrooms from Rochester to Portland: genuine interest in other people (Neri "deliberately" used his personal charm to win souls), cheerfulness (said Neri: "A cheerful and happy spirit attains perfection much sooner than a melancholy one."), being a good listener, talking in terms of the other person's interests. As for being a good listener, the Apostle of Rome not only paid careful attention to individual penitents but organized a kind of club, the famous Oratory, where his disciples did all the talking (about religious matters) while he only filled in the lulls. An adept in the art of talking shop, Neri amazed the doctors, lawyers, and other professional men and tradesmen of Rome, by his familiarity with their work.

These virtues turn the soul outward, away from itself, and provide that measure of altruism essential for peace of mind. They prevent us from watching the pot, thus keeping it from boiling. With them we include patience with the faults of others as well as with our own, and the charming knack of bringing out latent qualities by honest, timely praise and encouragement. This latter virtue characterized St. Peter Canisius.

45

In 1517, the year Martin Luther left the Church, Peter Canisius was baptized into it in the Netherlands. He became one of the first Jesuits from Northern Europe and spent the best part of his life (1549–1597) undoing the damage inflicted by the Reformation. Canisius was an important man: "educator of youth, founder of numerous colleges, missionary, popular preacher, reformer of the clergy, organizer, and upholder of his own order, adviser to princes and theologians in the diets of the Empire and at the Council of Trent, papal nuncio, publicist, eminent catechist."[8]

Yet he was never too busy to encourage others to serve Jesus' cause as their talents directed. To an aspiring young writer named William van der Lindt (or Lindanus), the saint wrote a winning letter, brimful of tact and wise counsel. Lindanus had just written a work excoriating the Vulgate version of the Bible which the Council of Trent had recently termed the "authentic" version of the Word of God. At the time, all of Europe was crying out for books defending the truths of Christ against the bludgeoning of heresy. But bumptious Lindanus, in the manner of the young, preferred to cut down a tree rather than grow one. Not wishing to break the youth's spirit, Canisius diplomatically suggested that with his talent Lindanus might better write a book defending the faith since that was the need of the time. Carefully Canisius nurtured the youth's talent by encouragement and artful suggestions. One of the greatest reformers in the history of the Church treated the "wholly unimportant" youth as if all the world hung on his words. Such sincere interest and guidance helped William van der Lindt to become later a truly important writer.

Characteristic of saints is a keen appreciation of the efforts

---

[8] *The Ignatian Way to God* by A. Brou (Milwaukee, Wis.: The Bruce Publishing Co., 1952), p. 77.

of others. "Love thy neighbor" meant no fleeting, fickle emotion, but a persevering effort in the service of the one loved. A distinguished old professor at St. Benedict's College in Atchison, Kansas, once advised a student to write down all the things he thought requisite for peace of mind. Next day the young man returned to the priest's room with a long typewritten list beginning: Health, money, friends, popularity, success in business, good reputation, long life, knowledge. The kindly old priest looked at the list, then glanced over the rims of his glasses at the young man perched on the chair before him. He chuckled, "You're going in the wrong direction. For peace of mind, it isn't a question of what we *get*, it's a question of what we *give*. Give God and your fellow men the love and service they deserve. Then you'll have peace of mind." The old Benedictine glanced down at the floor, slapped the arm of his rocking chair, and roared out merrily, "Give your heart's love to Christ and His cause and you'll make joy serve you. God gave us peculiar vision for seeing happiness. If we look square at it, it vanishes. But if we look away, look toward the needs of others and try to help them, out of the corners of our eyes we will see the cherished peace of mind. And that glimpse will warm our hearts all our lives."

A doctor of philosophy who has had great success in counselling students at a midwestern university remarked that a vital, compelling motive is needed to spur men on to virtue. "It is not enough, I have found, simply to counsel love of God. There has got to be some profit involved. The love of humans for God cannot be presented as if *no* profit for humans was to be derived from it. Some say, 'Love God so much that even if you got no profit from it you would still love Him, totally for Himself.' That sounds wonderful, but it closes off one aspect of the truth, because you cannot love God without

47

profiting from it! The more you love God, the more you profit from it. If a person were to think otherwise, he would be to that extent stupid, and stupidity would not please God, especially in such fundamental issues as love of God and the welfare of our souls."

After three years preparing at Cambridge and Detroit a doctoral dissertation on the labor philosophy of Walter Reuther, a Belgian Jesuit commented on America's high standard of living. Said Father Jules de Mey: "Europeans see, and sometimes envy, your high standard of living. What they do not always see is the immense amount of hard work you Americans do to keep that standard high. You are intensely hard working, active, clever people. That explains the abundance of wealth. It is not just an accident."

The Mass has two aspects. It can be viewed as a gift (from God to us) or as the payment of a debt (by us to God). Peace of mind also has two aspects. It is a gift (from God) or an achievement (by the individual). It is in a sense like a salary: we must work and pray for it. But also like a bonus: God grants it when we are prepared. As Harold Ruopp has said, God's chosen people are really the people who choose God.

Peace of mind does not mean the absence of struggle, of suffering, but the presence of maturity of spirit empowering us to master the trials encountered. Fra Angelico left upon canvas and the masonry walls of convents the essence of tranquillity in hues that muted the shrill, discordant passage of events outside the cloister — and inside, too. In his famous Nativity spun of fine gold and indigo there is no hint of the crisis rending Christendom at the time the painter worked, with three rivals staking vociferous claims to the Papal throne, and an engulfing Islamic tide crashing at Christian Europe's eastern shore.

What we need is not escape from it all, but a fixed look at our needs. St. Paul made no bones about wanting surcease from his mysterious "thorn in the flesh," but we have no record that it was ever removed, or even blunted. The Apostle to the Gentiles with a perfervid candor in examining his conscience turned up the fact of God's help ("my grace is sufficient for you") as well as that of his own inadequacy. His weakness did not make him despair, but God's tender concern brought an exultant cry of joy to his lips which is caught and echoed in the Introit of the Mass on the Third Sunday of Advent: "Joy to you in the Lord at all times; once again I wish you joy" (Phil. 4:4). The individual, we all must learn, is not omnipotent; even when its yearning after complete self-direction is crushed, there is joy in the balm of the presence of God. The flower yields its perfume when it is crushed. Paul's litany of sufferings was not a dirge but a high-spirited, rousing victory march. For him "to live is Christ and to die is a prize to be won," for him to suffer is to "fill up the things that are wanting to Christ's passion."

Our joy will not begin only in heaven. We were meant to be happy on earth too. The kingdom of heaven is not completely ultratemporal, as the prophets of doom, chiliasts, puritans, and others seem to believe. It has already begun. "The kingdom of God . . . means rightness of heart, finding our peace and our joy in the Holy Spirit" (Rom. 14:17). How can a citizen of that exclusive kingdom be smothered by gloom and anxiety? A small boy was once asked by his aunt if he had any plans for the future. He answered seriously, "I want to be a priest, or a comedian." The aunt asked why those particular choices. "Because they make people happy," the lad said. He thought of God's kingdom and joy as like Siamese twins, incapable of being separated and nourishing one another

49

from the same Source. The priest does bring happiness to the human race since he is the human agency for the offering of Mass. Because joy requires peace of mind, a genuine Christian full of worry and frustration is a sad anomaly.

The Mass assists in bringing to light various disturbing factors inimical to true Christian serenity. Through the graces flooding from it, it acts after the manner of a psychiatrist, or rather, vice versa. The late Sigmund Freud (d. 1939) focused the attention of neurosis-nagged humanity on certain important realities outside the pale of conscious awareness. The reality of neuroses and their need for skilled treatment, greater understanding and toleration of mental illness, and a clinical method of treating mental patients have won for Freud tremendous notoriety. Freud was not the first to advert to the existence of powers in the human personality moving in shadowy realms outside conscious awareness. Paul, theologian par excellence of the infant Church, exclaimed: "My own actions bewilder me; what I do is not what I wish to do, but something which I hate." The eternal pitched battle between good and evil takes place on every level of life. "It is not the good my will prefers, but the evil my will disapproves, that I find myself doing."[9] Freud was the first to examine scientifically the nature and origins of the "dark forces" locked into the mind of man, bringing them under rational consideration.

The Mass brings a man face to face with his own conscience in the presence of God, and by its graces, its imagery, its symbols, its music, its whole panoply of liturgy it draws from a man stark, clear flashes of intuition. "I was away from the Church for 23 years," a brigadier general admitted, "and it began to look as if I would die away from it. What brought me back was a funeral I attended for a fellow officer, a Catholic.

---

[9] Rom. 7:15, 19,

I sat there, depressed by the black colors and the somber chanting. All of a sudden it hit me like a ton of brick. I would be lying there soon. Death was a reality. And so was hell. For 23 years I had been in turmoil, and blamed it all on religion and hell-fire. At that funeral Mass it dawned on me that everything the Church said was real and that by admitting it, and living accordingly, the turmoil would be over. Thank God, it is. I can't hear those words of the funeral Mass, *Dies irae,* day of wrath, day of terror, without telling God how grateful I am. I haven't been to a psychiatrist since."

Many Americans opposed the passage of a law outlawing Communism because, they argued, it would drive the Reds underground, hence make them harder to observe and control. When a man "outlaws" sin, i.e., by refusing to think about it or admit its evil, he simply drives that recognition underground, and there it becomes a source of mental agony, instead of a healthy motive for virtue, since it is outside conscious control. A clinical psychologist of long experience once told a priest, "Perhaps not all mental conflicts take their origin in the clash between spirit and flesh, or in a man's refusing to admit that there is such a clash or that the spirit has any claims on him. But enlightened consideration and admission of that conflict and humble efforts to solve it are a major step in achieving peace of heart. I find traces, in varying degrees, of an unresolved conflict of this sort in many of the patients I treat. I usually try to persuade the Catholics to go to confession first. Once this is done, much of the spade work of a cure is already completed."

Peace in the world ("peace on earth") is the sum total of the peace to be found in individual human hearts. And the individual's peace depends on his right adjustment of relationships with God. The Mass is one place where this adjustment can be made; it is God's couch of psychoanalysis at which He, like a divine Socrates, leads us by mystic maieutic to discover and damp the fiery forces within. The Mass presents us with a realizable ideal: the imitation of Jesus. A primary factor in all neurosis, psychologists say, is a conviction that one must achieve an idealized degree of glamour or success, or else! The victim feels that he faces annihilation if he fails. On this delusion neurosis feeds. If the image of success to be sought is too farfetched, a nervous breakdown may result when the individual sees he can never attain it. The answer: a sensible, clear-cut image, one within reach. For the Christian, of course, that image is Christ. The Mass presents Christ as model for imitation. He is the Victim showing us how to suffer and make suffering worthwhile. "Yours is to be the same mind which Christ Jesus showed."[10] Our nobility of spirit is patterned off that of our Lord. "Him would I learn to know, and the virtue of His resurrection, and what it means to share his sufferings, moulded into the pattern of his death."[11] Even our suffering is patterned after Christ's: "Rejoice, when you share in some measure the sufferings of Christ."[12] So much is Jesus our image that Paul can say, "You are to be rooted in him, built up on him,"[13] and again, "ordering your lives in Christ Jesus our Lord, according to the tradition you have received of him."[14]

We can never *be* Christ. That would be an unrealizable image. To strive for that would be to strive for the impossible. But we can be *like* Him. Grace makes this possible, and the Mass above all makes grace ours. Grace is inseparable from peace of mind. St. Paul in all his letters wishes his readers

---

[10] Phil. 2:5.
[11] *Ibid.*, v. 10.
[12] 1 Pet. 4:13.
[13] Coloss. 2:7.
[14] *Ibid.*, v. 6.

grace and peace, the two terms being closely allied.[15] Sometimes the two terms seem almost interchangeable. In chapter five, verse fourteen, of his first epistle, St. Peter, according to the Greek text, says, "Peace be to all of you." According to the Latin: "Grace be to all of you." Grace enables us to make ourselves into a true and accurate image of Jesus by giving us such a share in His own life and powers. As the principal outpouring of the grace of God, the holy Mass must be the foundation of whatever peace of mind we will achieve in this life.

"Why pray when you can worry?" asks a sardonic billboard atop a Pentecostal temple. Let the perfectionist, grasping at an impossible image of success, go to Mass: it is the perfect form of worship. Let the worrywart go to Mass: it is more powerful than his peptic-ulcer-producing anxiety. Worry is chronic apprehensiveness over past, present, and future. The Mass can put an end to worry. It takes care of the past, the present, and the future. The past: "by this oblation the Lord . . . pardons wrongdoings and sins, even grave ones." The present: "through the Mass we may obtain mercy and find grace to help in time of need."[16] The future: says Father Sanchez, "we gain from holy Mass so firm a hope of the future life that supernatural faith is needed in order to believe it at all."

Someone has said that a good way of getting a certain feeling is to act as if we already had it. To achieve peace of mind, act as if we already possessed it. If we go to Mass often, we will have it. There we will pray for it from God,

---

[15] E.g., Coloss. 1:3; Phil. 1:2; Eph. 1:2; Gal. 1:3; Rom. 1:7; Cor. 1:3; 2 Cor. 1:2; 1 Thess. 1:1; 2 Thess. 1:2; 1 Tim. 1:2; 2 Tim. 1:2; Titus 1:4; and Philemon 1:3. Only in the letter to the Hebrews does Paul fail to open by wishing to his readers grace and peace.

[16] Roy Deferrari, *The Sources of Catholic Dogma* (St. Louis: B. Herder Book Co., 1957), p. 289. Council of Trent, sess. 22, chap. 2 (Denz. 940).

through His Son. We will pray with our Lady, close as usual to her Son in the unbloody Sacrifice of Calvary. It was she who spotted the embarrassment of bride and groom at Cana and asked of her Son His first miracle. Those of us who lack peace of mind through want, not of wine, but of trust and humble acquiescence, can pray through Mary: "Give to your household, O Lord, the gift of heavenly grace. Mary's giving birth to Christ was the beginning of our salvation. May the solemn festival of her Visitation give us an increase of peace. Through Christ our Lord."[17]

---

[17] Collect of the Mass, Feast of the Visitation, July 2.

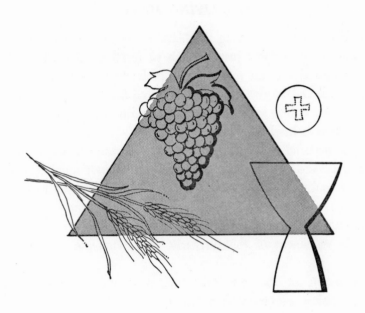

Bread and Wine and God

THE world of "things" around us — how important it is to God! He made it important. A body He took from that material world was the instrument of His sacred passion and death. The Blood of Christ, as St. Peter says, was the price of our redemption. Four of the seven sacraments have some material sign: water for baptism, oil for confirmation and extreme unction, bread and wine for the Eucharist.

Material things, even simple ones, can save human life. During an H-bomb test near Eniwetok atoll, the shock wave from the blast knocked out a radar antenna meant to guide

Air Force planes observing the blast. An engineer fixed it with a metal coat hanger, just in time to recall a pilot who was mistakenly flying out to sea — and probably to his death. The old South Dakota country doctor repaired his battered Model-T Ford with baling wire, and it brought him to his patient in time to save his life.

The material in the Eucharist is simple bread and wine. And yet it is used by God as a means of the highest sanctification of the soul. God does not despise the world of matter; in fact, He has incorporated it into His system of sanctification. Perhaps tops on this list are bread and wine, called the "matter" of the sacrament of the Eucharist. Just what are bread and wine?

Members of the Air Transport Association boiled up a metaphysical brouhaha over the question: What is a sandwich? Limited to serving "sandwiches" on certain flights, some airlines had turned the pedestrian sandwich into a lavish meal. Perhaps everyone is entitled, as a Swissair spokesman reportedly said, to his own concept of sandwich. But things are not so imprecise regarding bread and wine. We know what they are.

A chemist for the Manor Bread Company in Kansas City explained that wheat flour is a marvelous material containing many enzymes, alpha-amylase, beta-amylase, gluten. As soon as these components are in contact with water, they perform some wonderful, intricate chemical changes! The alpha-amylase breaks down the starch and the beta-amylase changes some of the starch into sugar (a process called "saccharifying," i.e., making sugar out of). Bacterial action in the flour produces other intricate changes resulting in aroma and flavors characteristic of bread. The process is so complicated, in fact, that it has not as yet been wholly studied.

Some of the many gluten changes, now being analyzed in further detail, are fully known. Gluten is both carbohydrate and protein. It, with the rest of the wonderful contents of wheat flour, is present in just the right quantity to result in that common, everyday staple: bread. Enzymes are not usually living; some, called "biochemical catalysts," are living. These enzymes, which speed up chemical reactions, play such a dominant part in the chemistry of life that one chemist remarked, "It is almost impossible to imagine the synthesis of a living thing without the help of the enzyme." Just about everything that happens in an organism is governed by this special class of protein called "enzyme."

Wheat flour contains all this. Add water, and presto! Bread forms. A series of reactions ensues more complicated than that of the most advanced electronic "brain." Baking does not make bread; bread is formed through the natural propensities of water to "marry" with wheat flour in the chemical ritual already partially described. Baking arrests these processes.

We have bread, then, before baking. "Most people," a moral theologian explained, "think that dough becomes bread when it is baked. This is not true. The dough is already bread, before it is baked. Theologians, following the common view, always held that unbaked dough is invalid matter for the consecration of the Mass. Chemically, though, and really, the dough is bread already, thanks to certain chemical changes."

"Ever since I studied chemistry in high school," a student exclaimed, "I wondered how it could be said that 'bread' was changed, since I always thought that the wafer of the host was only some flour in round, stuck-together form. And I was afraid to ask. . . ."

That is farthest from the truth! The flour, as soon as it is introduced to the water, strikes up an intimate friendship, a number of chemical changes are induced, and in a trice, bread! A host that has been pulverized is not flour but pulverized bread.

Many of the Eastern Rites (e.g., the Chaldean Liturgy, the Liturgy of the Copts) use leavened bread in the Mass. How does it differ from unleavened bread? The yeast "raises" the bread by forming bubbles of carbon dioxide gas which carbonate and lighten the bread while all the other (important and breadmaking) processes are going on due to the combination of flour and water. The yeast blows bubbles of carbon dioxide (CO_2) into the dough. When the dough is baked, the carbon dioxide is driven off by the heat, while the shells of the bubbles remain, fixed in their configurations. Both leavened and unleavened bread are equally bread; the leavened bread has, in addition, many holes in it which used to be occupied by the carbon dioxide.

This, then, is the marvelous stuff that Jesus took into His hands, blessed, and broke, saying, "This is my body." Sister Helena at St. Rose's Residence in a midwest city usually makes the mixture of flour and water the day before and lets it stand overnight. Sisters Cabrini and Annunziata at an orphanage in the same city say it takes 45 minutes to mix the flour and water, and then they leave the mixture to stand for fifteen more minutes while the waffle-iron-like oven heats. While Sisters Olga and Annunziata are mixing flour and water in their convent kitchens, all the alpha-amylase and beta-amylase and gluten changes are transforming the erstwhile flour-and-water mixture into true bread. Bread is forming "automatically" because of the nature God planted in the flour, formed out on the wind-swept plains of Kansas or in the Nebraska sunshine, through the long summer and the harvest, waiting until the will and words of a priest would one day annihilate it in perfect sacrifice. And more! Change it into the Body and Blood of Christ.[1]

Christ chose, for the sacrament of His body and blood, the two most universal foods: bread and wine. Wine, the "living blood of the grape" (André L. Simon), with its long, rich history, in the Mass achieves peak adventure by being turned into the flesh and blood of the Son of God. How fitting that God should have picked wine! — wine, dating back at least to 2400 B.C. in Egypt — wine, praised by Horace (65–8 B.C.), who mentions an old and choice brand of Falernian wine in Carmina No. 3 (*interiore nota Falerni*) — wine, called the "most healthful and hygienic of all beverages" by Louis Pasteur. No steak is adequate without burgundy. Cheese demands its port; seafood its glass of mellow, golden sauterne. Wine is the universal mealtime drink of Latin peoples.

This is what God chose to benefit the supernatural health of mankind in the sacrament of the Eucharist. Wine-become-Communion aids the hygiene of holiness. It puts the finishing touch on human life, nourishing all the needs of the soul. Because of wine, Great Britain became a great sea power, increasing her ships under Edward III so as to reap more profit from wine trade with Bordeaux. Wine-become-Christ's-Blood builds diffident, fainthearted Milquetoasts into courageous *caballeros* of Christ, turns craven sensualists into models of terrifying asceticism.

What is this "wine," native of Egypt and Asia Minor? What is this many-hued liquid which captured hearts around the Mediterranean, in Greece, Rome, France, and all western Europe? What is this wine that conquered more devastatingly than Caesar the Gauls?

---

[1] Annihilation, or "creation backward," does not take place in the Mass. The substance of bread and wine is not reduced to nothing but altogether changed into Christ's body and blood. This is called "transubstantiation."

It is another item in the catalogue of material things chosen by God for high destiny. It is a product of the grape (*Vitis vinifera*) and results from a process called "fermentation." Judith, the "valiant woman," "bemused" Holofernes with wine before chopping off his head. Wine was "blamed" for the Apostles' terrific preaching (Acts 2:13). St. Paul told Timothy that some wine would settle his stomach (1 Tim. 5:23). Wine starred at Cana.

As grapes ripen, their total acid content falls and sugar content rises, until at full maturity a pleasing balance obtains. Wine yeasts by a divinely planned "accident" gather on the skins of grapes as they ripen. When the grapes are crushed these yeasts speed up fermentation. Grape sugar is broken down into ethyl alcohol and carbon dioxide and a host of other substances (among others, succinic, lactic, acetic, and formic acids; pentose sugars, propionaldehyde, cinamaldehyde, vanillin, esters, nitrogen, enzymes, and vitamins). Fermentation is a natural process. It begins as soon as juice is crushed from grapes. Wineries control and perfect this process to guarantee maximum quality in all conditions.

God did not despise material creation, but chose it instead to convey Him to man. Survival, military experts say, depends on certain material things such as missiles and satellites. But the Mass beats these and remains, in the words of Father Frank Gartland, C.S.C., "the most marvellous victory which has been won over time and space." Speaking over the CBS "Church of the Air," Father Gartland called the Mass a "projection through time and space of the sacrifice of Christ upon the cross . . . the mystery of our redemption on Calvary daily renewed around the earth, circling it, uninterrupted for nineteen centuries, from altar to altar over countless orbits of divine grace."

Bread and wine are "matter" for the Mass. When bread is no longer bread, it is no longer fit for use in the Mass. So, with wine. Wine left for a length of time in contact with the air will turn sour. Certain bacteria (*mycoderma aceti*) engineer a union of oxygen and alcohol to form acetic acid. When this change is fairly complete, wine is substantially changed, and has become vinegar.

The Mass deserves nothing but the best in vestments, vessels, and in bread and wine, too. Wineries, most of them employing their own chemists, are very particular about their product, according to the Wine Institute of San Francisco, and use severely controlled methods of fermentation, cooling, and aging to keep the quality high. The Church is equally concerned, since the very Mass depends upon it. Briefly, the wine must be (1) from grapes, (2) unspoiled by bacteria (viz., not soured), (3) natural and not artificial, (4) produced from ripe grapes (in unripe grapes the sugar content is low, acid high, hence the wine would contain less alcohol), (5) a product of the first squeezing of the grapes, (6) containing alcohol not to exceed 20 per cent, and (7) unmixed with foreign substances in equal or greater quantities.[2]

This is the bread, this the wine, that make up the "matter" of the Holy Eucharist. God, who loves material things (He made them), adopts them, too, as part of His methods of redemption. Not least: bread and wine. Into the wine the priest pours a drop or two of water (the wine Christ used at the Last Supper had a small admixture of water). The mixture is symbolic of the human and divine natures of Christ; or of

---

[2] Cf. "Sacramental Altar Wine and Church Legislation" by Rev. Arthur L. McNeil, S.J., reprinted in *The Wine Review*, May, 1947, p. 10, June, 1947, pp. 8 and 28. Father McNeil's advice to pastors puzzling over Mass wine: Use wine made by religious or by wineries with letters of approval from the Ordinary of the diocese where the wine was made and bottled.

the water and blood that issued from the pierced side of the Savior; or of the union of Jesus with His Church, in which they become one (Mystical) Body, as water and wine become one physical reality, wine. The priest must add the water or commit mortal sin. Should he not do so, however, the Mass would still be valid.

The water, mixed with the wine, becomes wine and so is consecrated. The priest's will to consecrate, called "intention," according to the common view, reaches out some fifty or sixty feet to embrace bread and wine and cause their transubstantiation even at that distance, unless he expressly excludes them from his will. Beyond that distance bread and wine are not "physically present," hence, not "consecratable." Moreover, the priest's will to convert bread and wine into Christ's body and blood must fix itself upon *this* bread and *this* wine.

The priest's intention may be actual: as he pronounces the words of consecration he is conscious of his desire to change the bread and wine. Or it may be virtual: he had the desire to effect that transubstantiation, and it is because of it that he is celebrating Mass now, even though he is not now conscious of that desire. Either of these *intentiones* is sufficient for a good Mass. If his *intentio* were merely intentional, if it no longer exercised any influence over the acts of the priest, the consecration would not be valid, there would be no Mass, e.g., a priest in delirium of fever pronounces the sacred words over the bread and wine. No consecration would take place.

It was not surprising when Anglican Archbishop Arthur M. Ramsey of Canterbury, at a Eucharistic Congress in London, pointed out the "urgent need today for the doctrines of the Presence and the Sacrifice of the Mass." Though the Anglicans no longer have valid priests (hence no Mass, no consecration of bread and wine), still they realize that God's concern must be their concern; that bread and wine attain the deepest significance for man when they become, by a startling act of divine mercy exercised through the free and determined act of a priest, God's body. He made them His, that we might, by making them our own, make Him our own. When bread and wine are changed into Christ, we eat them that He might change us, bit by bit, into Himself.

Evil is not just something *done,* it is something thought or wished. If we can share in a man's guilt by rejoicing in his sin, so can we share in his reward by being glad for his virtues. A whole new world of merit is opened to us, though we never leave the home of our own mind.

There are degrees of guilt incurred by sinners, depending on how closely they co-operate in a sinful act. The publisher, printer, and editor of obscene literature incur very grave guilt. Linotypists and proofreaders may do their jobs if they can't make a living any other way; otherwise, they too are guilty. The mechanic who services the presses which print this literature needs a less serious reason to perform his task than the proofreader and linotypist.

There are degrees, too, in the extent to which we can co-operate in good deeds. At Mass, the "most holy and divine" of all good deeds (Council of Trent), there is one group that co-operates more closely than others in an unsung way. It is an ingenious group, too. In the Cathedral at Managua, Nicaragua, Bishop Matthew Niedhammer, O.F.M.Cap., solemnly intoned the *Gloria.* As the choir completed the glorious hymn of praise the Bishop went to the *scamnum* and sat down. The altar boys had been carefully trained for months in the intricate ceremony. "Keep your hands folded," they were told repeatedly. As they sat down for the *Gloria,* it was found there was one chair too few. The acolyte without a chair unabashedly bowed to the Bishop and disappeared into the sacristy. Moments later he returned to the sanctuary. His hands were still folded piously. The missing chair was balanced expertly on top of his head!

How important the altar boys are! Their parents also co-operate, it is true, in the Mass. Chiefly by offering it along with the priest. But in more remote ways, too; by contributing money which buys the paraphernalia needed, by raising the wheat and grapes, making the bread and wine, building the church and the seminaries where priests are formed, and by contributing good young men to become priests. But the altar boys co-operate more closely than this in the Mass, by answering the prayers, moving the book and veil, and bringing up the water and wine at the Offertory and after the Communion.

Somehow youngsters realize that by serving they are sharing more completely in the riches of the Holy Sacrifice. A young priest in the diocese of Amarillo, Texas, said that he owed his priesthood to his being an altar boy. "I became interested in the Mass and in the priesthood while serving in my parish church. I got close to the priests and saw what fine men they were. The lessons they taught me in countless ways, and most importantly the graces of the many Masses I served, combined to bring me finally to God's altar as a priest."

The Church knows how important the altar boys are and has legislated regarding their part in the Mass (Canon 813). Habitually saying Mass without a server is a serious matter, it is true, although a priest can do it "per modum actus," that is, *occasionally*. And even if a priest is going to be "habitually" without a server, he can get permission to say Mass without one.

"I was shocked," remarked a member of a parish in Erie, Pennsylvania, "when the pastor said Mass one weekday morning without a server. I had the mistaken idea that it is a sin always for a priest to say Mass without a server. And I was wrongly shocked to see it done. And of course how wise the Church is in this. Wouldn't it be a shame for us to lose that Mass simply because an altar boy forgot to set his alarm clock!"

The lady is right, of course. The server is important, as a close co-operator with the priest in the offering of Mass, but not so necessary that the priest cannot say Mass *per modum actus*, and this with no sin at all. As the famous moral theologian, Father Capello says, the priest can do this for the reason that he loves the Mass and does not wish to lose a single opportunity to offer it (*etiam devotionis causa*).

And so, God has thoroughly involved Himself in the world, by creating it, rescuing it from nothingness, and continuing that support from inside the world. Total dedication of God to His creation! He became man! He became flesh (*sarx* is the word St. John uses), despite the total lack of parity between fleshmeat (the idea connoted by *sarx*) and God. A star provided outdoor advertising for the Babe in the manger, wood became crib and cross, and it was on wood He chose to work for 30 years. He worked miracles of healing with mud, then spiritual miracles of grace with water and wine, with oil, with words. He chose weak humans to continue His sacramental existence. Moreover, tousle-headed altar boys, eyes sandy with sleep, play a part in this extraordinary drama. And they often recognize the value of what they are doing. At a midwest Benedictine college priests gather annually to make their retreat. Neighborhood boys are recruited to serve Masses each morning, and rewarded afterward with breakfast. One of them was heard to remark to a companion as they trudged toward the cafeteria, "I *only* got to serve one Mass this morning."

God's coming into it has ennobled the *whole* world.

Sticking to It

(SCENE: *A broadcasting booth in heaven. Seated at a table behind microphones are three figures: an interrogator with black hair slicked away from his forehead and a prize fighter's jaw, a young girl of innocence and beauty, and a grizzled old man with weather-beaten face. The interrogator speaks to the old man.*)

How do you do. You are St. Peter, the first pope, I understand.
Yes, I was the first pope.
I understand you were crucified with your head downward. Is that correct?
That is correct.
Why did you select such an unusual way to be crucified?
I did that because Jesus Christ was crucified with His head up,

66

and I am not worthy to suffer in the same way, because in my foolishness I denied my Master.

What gave you the terrific strength and courage to be crucified willingly in the first place?

When I considered that life on earth is only a short one, and the next eternal, it was not very difficult. But most of all, I had the Lord right with me through the Mass and Holy Communion. They gave me more than enough strength to be a martyr.

(The interviewer then turns to the young girl.) How do you do, St. Agnes. I understand that you had your head chopped off? That must have been a terrifying thing!

Well, it was terrifying. But I had the strength of God with me through the Mass and Holy Communion.

Yes, but it must have been a terrible ordeal.

I may say that there are some advantages to having one's head chopped off.

Advantages! Good heavens! What do you mean?

You have heard that "two heads are better than one." Well, I would reword that saying and put it this way, "None is better than one." I might have grown up and lived a very ordinary life and even might have missed heaven entirely. Having my head chopped off, I merited an eternity of reward with God in heaven. It gave me a chance to prove my love for my dear Savior who was crucified for me. He died for me. So I was given the chance to die for love of Him.

It's a remarkable thing for a twelve-year-old girl. Is it true that the handcuffs slipped off your wrists because your hands were so tiny?

Oh yes (with a merry laugh), that's right. But even if they hadn't I wouldn't have minded. Christ became a slave for me. Now it was my turn.

Just where did the whole terrible trial begin?

At the temple of some fictitious Roman goddess named Minerva. They wanted me to burn some grains of incense in adoration of this phony goddess. I wouldn't do it.

But at the cost of your life!

We weren't going to live forever — on earth. It was ironic, wasn't it, that it should have begun at the altar to the goddess of wisdom. Pagan wisdom it was, but not the wisdom of God. I gave up a few years of life, yes. But look what I gained!

Just what did you gain, St. Agnes? Could you sum up for our audience, in a few words, what you had waiting for you when you lost your life?

In a few words! Oh, I couldn't do that. There was another martyr, Paul was his name, who got a glimpse.

What was his reaction, St. Agnes?

He could only gasp, "Eye hath not seen nor ear heard the things the Lord has prepared for those who love Him."

Thanks to you both, St. Peter and St. Agnes, for appearing on our show this evening. And now, ladies and gentlemen, I return you to the studio in New York City.

* * *

POPULAR tunes, automobile stylings, dry cereals, and political platforms come and go with such rapidity that one can't keep up with them from one year to the next. Sometimes the virtues, too, are chucked aside as obstructing progress. So faith in changeless principles of right falls victim to our erratic quest of the kingdom of selfdom. Both St. Peter and St. Agnes, along with the millions of other martyrs and saints, prove our need for perseverance. They point out, too, where we can get it. Item: the Mass gives perseverance.

The Mass is a constant, keen reminder to do good. Sometimes the answer to vice is that simple. Without the pretentious argot of pseudo-psychoanalysis the recommendation of St. Paul is rather refreshing. To hijackers and kindred spirits he remarks candidly, "The man who was a thief must be a thief no longer" (Eph. 4:28). The Mass says that — and gives the power to *do* it.

"Psychiatrists," one of them has commented, "may sometimes read more into human motives than reality warrants. When American vacationers cram the nation's highways bumper to bumper during the summer, rushing headlong to relax in some spot abandoned by other vacationers who are hurrying elsewhere, students of the psyche have a field day. I recall one of my colleagues who said that the insane, grass-is-greener-in-the-other-yard feeling that is driving Americans from one vacation mecca to the next is an index of a certain lack of inner stability. That may be true. Perhaps we feel we lack something, and this tempestuous tourism is our way of finding it. But then on the other hand, maybe we Americans just *like* to travel."

Maybe sinners just *want* to sin. Just *like* to sin. Would that explain the cryptic remark of Paul, "Be a thief no longer"? Sin, unlike tourism, is not seasonal. What we need is a year-round antidote to it, the Mass.

In theology much is said about perseverance, with reference chiefly to our continuing in the grace of God until our death. The Church has given repeated assurance that we can get the gift of final perseverance if we humbly ask it of almighty God. Though we must not "feel assured of this gift (of final perseverance) with an absolute certitude," we all ought to have "most secure hope in the help of God. For unless men are unfaithful to his grace, God will bring the good work to perfection, just as he began it, working both the will and the performance."[1] Later on the same Council of Trent condemned anyone who taught that with God's special help it is still impossible for a man in the state of grace to live his holy Christian life to the very last breath.[2]

Perseverance is a gift, not something we merit in the strict sense of the word. It is a bonus, not a wage; an extra dividend, not interest due; given by God out of mercy, not out of justice.

---

[1] *The Church Teaches*, translated by the Jesuit Fathers of St. Mary's College, St. Marys, Kansas (St. Louis Mo.: B. Herder Book Co., 1955), p. 238. Trent, Session 6 (June 21, 1546, to Jan. 13, 1547), chap. 13, Denz. 806.

[2] *Ibid.* (Trent, Canon 22, Denz. 832), p. 245.

I once talked to a famous old theologian at a school in Kansas, and I asked him what he considered the most difficult thing of all in his career. He meditated quietly a few moments and then replied, "Just staying with it for so many years. Just being on the job for half a century." I expressed amazement, and the old priest continued, "Yes, this obstacle of long-time-ness is a real problem in human relations. It is a test among all people of sincerity and strength of character. All recognize that it is easy to do something difficult for a few moments or a few days or, even, for a few years. But to carry on through years and years, with the same steadfastness of purpose and unflinching resolve — that is recognized at once as something especially worthy of merit." I asked him if there was a word for this obstacle which time puts in the way of persevering. "Yes, we can call it diuturnity. That's an abstract noun from the Latin *diu* meaning 'a long time.' Its meaning, then, would be 'long-timeness.' It is a real test of gumption. There are many who start out gaily on a job, a trip, an enterprise. There are few who carry it out."

The lavish celebrations and publicity given on silver and golden jubilees attest to the instinctive value people attach to perseverance. Yet, with the assurance given by the Mass, we need not face the future fearfully or with quavering hearts. "We are confident even over our afflictions," St. Paul said, including the affliction of long-timeness, "knowing well that affliction gives rise to endurance, and endurance (i.e., perseverance) gives proof of our faith" (Rom. 5:3, 4). Keeping at it, in the most humdrum daily tasks — like the Samaritan stranger described in the Gospel of the Mass for the twelfth Sunday after Pentecost! There he goes, hurrying along on his flop-eared mule, understandably in a hurry to get out of a very unfriendly country. Then he sees the wounded Jew, dresses his wounds, and carries him on his own animal to the nearest shelter, where he pays the equivalent of two days' wages. We do not read anywhere that he expected to be (or was) cordially treated by this or any other Jew afterward. It was simply a question of helping a man in need. He provided first-aid, transportation, and a room, with a promise to come back if more money was needed for room rental or food. This is our model for perseverance in doing good: because it pleases God and brings us nearer Him, whether we are applauded for it and those we help grateful or not.

"There are many who start out gaily on a job," the old Kansas theologian had said, "few who carry it out." It is not Edith Stein the new convert whom we admire. It is rather Edith Stein who persevered in her life of virtue despite terrific tension and gnawing trials. The same is true of all converts, cradle converts, infants converted from original sin to original grace at baptism.

Christ summed up His estimate of steadfastness as a virtue in His statement that not every man who says "Lord! Lord!" (with initial bursts of enthusiasm) will be saved, but only the man who perseveres to the end (i.e., overcomes the hurdle of diuturnity). Wilhelm Liebknecht (1826–1900), one of the founders of socialism in Germany and a disciple of Karl Marx, remarked that one of Marx's favorite sayings was a verse from Dante, *Segui il tuo corso, e lascia dir le genti*, "Follow your course and let people say what they will." (Marx quotes this toward the end of the Preface of *Das Capital*.) This peppy epigram, filled with more than a gram of sense, is aphorism enough for us Christians, who have as model the rampant (in the sense of prevailing unbridled) Christ, ruling the lives and hearts and destinies of men from His escutcheon of the cross; a suffering yet gentle Christ, who died in the face of the incredulous dunning of passersby, speaking for humanity.

"The price of progress is trouble," grunted harassed Charles E. Wilson, one-time president of General Motors and ex-Secretary of Defense of the U. S. "And I must be making lots of progress." Progress in the Christian life will involve trouble, too, from the devil, the world, and one's own laziness and complacence. Jacques Maritain has commemorated the painter Georges Rouault (1871–1958) for his "heroic perseverance" in disregarding the snickers of critics who said his work was inconsequential and who dubbed him a madman. The great convert artist persevered. Born in a cellar on May 27, 1871, while troops from Versailles shelled the Paris suburb of Belleville, Rouault stayed at his easel and canvas to become one of the most influential of modern French artists. Perhaps his most famous work is the *Miserere,* a series of fifty-eight prints in black and white dealing with the perennial character of Christ's passion. His own artistic life and the life of us all is defined in the title of the last of these fifty-eight plates: It is the face of Christ, agony over, Beatitude begun: "It is with His stripes that we are healed."

Every man's life is the work of his hands on the canvas of his soul, in the bright colors of the virtues, or the ugly daubs of vice. Only the Mass can give us integrity and grit enough to paint on, when everyone hollers "quit!" and hands shake. But we persevere, until our masterpiece is done: the image of the Glorious and Crucified, etched there forever on our soul.

A small investment magazine titled *Your Tomorrow* told the story (June, 1958) of the misplaced data. The superintendent of the plant where the magazine is printed couldn't locate the important material. Finally he called up and said jubilantly, "I found it!" "Where was it?" "In the back of my file I have a folder marked 'Look Here When You Are Sunk.' Your data couldn't possibly be in that folder, but this morning I looked. And there it was!"

The Mass should be marked, "Look Here When You Are Discouraged." When you want to quit, to give up, to give in to temptation, to stop trying, go to Mass. The Mass is God's answer to the long haul of life. It makes difficult things easy, impossible things surmountable.

There are physical and psychical drawbacks to steadfastness in humans. Our bodies wear down and our attention tends to be deflected. The view we first have of a plan, a goal, a career, does not show all the later developments; it may not include the hardships which progress along the way to achievement will bring into our path. The hands poising a scalpel for its swift, precise sally had first to tie endless knots and master intricate techniques before piercing living tissue. Many a longing for a pilot's wings has gone glimmering during back-breaking obstacle courses and memory-breaking classes in aerology, navigation, and engines. As a man or woman undertakes the voyage of matrimony, its turning horizon often brings up icebergs of misunderstanding, hurricanes of anger, and gray fogs of tedium that hadn't been anticipated in the exciting putting out to sea. A Kansas City fireman who almost daily tools a massive Pirsch fire engine through teeming traffic sighed over his family responsibilities. "I never realized what a tough job it is to bring up kids. Give me a four-alarm fire any day."

Perseverance becomes more concerned with the obstacle of long-timeness or diuturnity as more people live to be older. More years mean more heartaches, more broken dreams, more frustration — but also more chances to gain grace, more avenues to supernatural perfection opened, more insights into the divine goodness. "Old age is a precious gift from God," explained an elderly bishop. "I savor each moment from His hand, I count each one a new eternity because each single grace deposited to my account in successive instances is in itself a little eternity."

That was the outlook of lean, lantern-jawed Jean Baptiste Lamy, who threaded the wastes of New Mexico on his tired pony, saddle bags stuffed with a few items of clothing and bread, crackers, and hard-boiled eggs. Down the valley of the Rio Grande the first bishop of New Mexico clopped, his frontiersman's eye carefully scanning arroyos and distant horizons for signs of prowling Comanches. As a schoolboy Lamy and his chum Joseph Machebeuf, in 1867 to be bishop of the woolly, mile high diocese of Denver, had adopted a motto from the patois of their native Auvergne. It was *Latsin pas!* "Never give up!" From the time Lamy made his way down the gangplank of a battered vessel at Galveston, Texas, with a commission from the Holy Father Pius IX in his suitcase naming him Vicar Apostolic of New Mexico, until he died in the high-walled square room in the Archbishop's house in Santa Fe on February 13, 1888, at age 74, he had kept that motto in view. *Latsin pas!*[3] He drew his strength from the Mass, whether he offered it on the sunburnt prairies of New Mexico, the lush San Luis Valley of Colorado, or on a snow-covered hillside in Arizona.

"The man who has faith in me enjoys eternal life," said Jesus to the Jews as they complained over His demand that they eat His flesh and drink His blood. (See Jn. 6:41 ff.) No mere fly-by-night faith will do, but a tried and tested, long-term faith, incarnate in a lifetime of loving service like that of Bishop Lamy. The Gospel of the Mass for Wednesday after

[3] Paul Horgan, "Jean Baptiste Lamy," *The Month*, Vol. 18, No. 4 and Vol. 18, No. 5 (October and November, 1957) (London: Longmans, Green and Co., publisher of *Month*). This article was from pages 203 to 214 in the October issue and pp. 282 to 292 in the November issue.

Pentecost does not merely sound out Christ's dictum that faith fathers eternal life; it reminds us that the Mass gives the means for believing and for living in tune with that belief. And for a lifetime.

Body weariness hampers the starflight of genius as well as the plod of ordinary common sense. The great Finnish composer Jean Sibelius, who died in 1958, chuckled; his great, shining cranium atop the egg-cup collar, tilted merrily and the massive, hearty face descended in ample folds down over chin and collar, ending somewhere under a white waistcoat. To Dr. Antonio Brico, the director of a Businessman's Symphony orchestra, Sibelius said, "I have a great many things to say in music, things more beautiful than anything I've yet done. But I'm too tired to go through the labor of putting the notes down." At times the thought of persevering in virtue has similar repercussions. After Ignatius of Loyola put aside his soldier's boots and sword for a pilgrim's weeds, he very nearly despaired over the thought of persevering in virtue for another forty or fifty years.

The goal is worth the effort of persevering. Christ continually turned the thoughts of His disciples to the reward in store. And St. Paul in turn said, "Let us fix our eyes on Jesus, the origin and crown of all faith" (Hebr. 12:2). We are entered in a race and must run "with all endurance" (*ibid.*, verse 1), patterning ourselves on Christ. The Christian searching for fresh contact with Christ in each day's experience has no fear of the hobgoblin of Time with its ominous ticking countdown for the soul's launching into eternity. "There is no need to fear those who kill the body," says the Gospel of the Mass of St. Polycarp (January 26). No need to fear brainwashing or guillotine, social ostracism or the gibbet, poverty or old age: these only attack the body, shell of the soul, pod of God's indwelling. They cannot touch the control-center, and it is in this control-center that the key to perseverance lies. In the powerful faculties of the soul, the energy of the Mass sets in motion the machinery of the human will, impervious to any power on earth. The winning of heaven may not always be full of thrills and exhilaration, but it is full of the deepest satisfaction, prelude to final enjoyment of God.

"The men who are sowing in tears will reap, one day, with joy. Mournful enough they go, but with seed to scatter; trust me, they will come back rejoicing, as they carry their sheaves with them" (Tract, Mass of St. Agatha, February 5).

"This is primary," a student counselor said in a talk to his high school boys. "The virtue of steadfastness has got to be developed. And since it has to be, it can be. God never demands the impossible. It is within the power of the human will and body to overcome the hurdle of long-timeness, to cultivate stick-to-it-iveness. Necessity, after all, is the mother of invention. Southern rice growers were confined by the nature of the land to grow crops in a small area of tide-swampland. They became the best, most scientific farmers in the South, being forced to reclaim swamps and develop the use of high-potency fertilizers. Our model is Christ. And what His life provides us with as archetype, His death, re-enacted in the Mass, enables us to imitate in our own day-to-day lives."

One student chaplain recommended these special means of attaining steadfastness. "Habitual adherence to our duty, no matter what allurements creep in. Unflinchingly facing problems with firm reliance on God. A great trust in the loving care of the Blessed Virgin Mary. Careful direction of our attention and instantaneous repulsion of thoughts contrary to our purpose. All these have to be used."

Jaffa, planted in whitewashed stolidness on the edge of a

cliff overlooking the Mediterranean, offered to a Jewish shepherd of the year 6 B.C. attractions that the barren grazing fields around the poky village of Bethlehem couldn't supply. But if certain shepherds had thrown down their staves and set their faces toward the coastlands, they would not have been in the fields near Bethlehem to receive God's invitation from a choir of angels, asking them to attend the first audience of the newborn King of kings. Perseverance always pays off.

The tendency in all of us to ask, "How can I get out of this?" when faced with a problem, to quit when the going gets rough, is the result of several factors. One of them is advertising. The ad man, dubbed "Freud in a Grey Flannel Suit" by John Sisk,[4] is skilled in MR (= Motivation Research), a new technique among the tart, perhaps Tartuffian hucksters. Today's atomic ad man, armed with MR, probes the human psyche, studying what causes the consumer to buy, and then appealing to these hidden motives that even the customer isn't aware of. "One of the by-products of advertising," commented a professor of sociology at the University of Detroit, "is to convince us that since everything is made easy by some gadget or other, *all* our problems should be made easy of solution." It is evident from the gospel of the ad men that the drudgery has been taken out of everything, from washday to childbearing. Hence, nothing difficult is left. If a difficulty crops up, we instinctively look for an easy way out.

Advertising alone cannot be blamed for this tendency which antedates the days of LSMFT and Irium. One day in Capharnaum Jesus said that He was going to give His followers His body to eat and His blood to drink, and that this food would give them eternal life, starting right now in this sleepy Oriental

---

[4] John Sisk, "Freud in a Grey Flannel Suit," *America* (August 10, 1957), pp. 480–482.

village. After that "many of his disciples went back to their old ways, and walked no more in his company."[5] When something difficult of belief was presented to them, something only faith in Jesus could make them accept, these men glanced archly at one another, gesticulated, balked. Their solution to this embarrassing puzzle was not to face it, to pretend they hadn't heard the sighing of the Holy Spirit in their souls. It is true that long-timeness or diuturnity cannot be made easy, for us any more than for the disciples. The revolving of the earth is not speeded up or slowed down. Literally, time marches on.

A man who must trudge through long years will necessarily win a few callouses on his feet and cough the dust of the road. He reaches one of life's horizons only to find another ahead, tops a ridge of study only to discover another and loftier one looming, turns each bend in the road to virtue only to find an unexpected detour pointing (it seems) away from the goal. But all roads of duty lead to God; His detour is a more direct route. And much of a man's success in persevering will depend on his outlook. How does he view perseverance in virtue? An employer tells the story of two young men not long in his organization, who were given identical jobs to do. A day or two later he inquired how they were doing. "I'm only half done," one said dourly. "I'm already half finished," the other replied with a cheery smile.

"Persevere!" scribbled young Peter Canisius in large capital letters in his theme book. That thought can be terrifying or consoling. Terrifying if we assess man's native staying power independently of the divine promise. Something of that terror, though subdued, found its way into the heart of Stephen Daedalus in James Joyce's *Portrait of the Artist As a Young*

---

[5] Jn. 6:67.

Man: Daedalus wondered at the "frail hold" the discipline and experience of the past had upon him, especially when he was tempted to commit sexual sin. Is our hold on decency and virtue (on God) really frail? Is it weak, anemic, emasculated, that hold, a hold no human agency can loose? Is that a frail hold? Only a man himself can abdicate his freedom in goodness by sin. No revolution can unseat his mastery of himself except the revolution of his own free choice.

Christ in the Mass helps us to look to a further horizon, cross another threshold, plow another furrow, begin a new chapter, close another day, smile again after tears. On the cross Jesus reached the pinnacle of redemption, and as if terrified by the thought of our being left alone He materialized His sacrifice in bread and wine and a priest's will and words. The Mass makes God's love and mercy more than ideas or raw concepts, refining them into working realities that will change our lives. "I may not be able to change the world," a former reporter with the Chicago *Daily News* remarked at a press convention, "but I can better inform it." We may not be able to change the world, but we can change *ourselves.* The Mass gives the needed strength. It is not just another work performed by man in holy association with God. When Michael du Bay taught that it was, at the University of Louvain, he was censured by St. Pius V in a bull "Ex omnibus afflictionibus," of October 1, 1567 (Denz. 1045). The Mass is a work of the God-Man: nothing else can account for its grandeur and power. In the Mass "the most sublime matters . . . lie hidden" (Denz. 943), and many of these mysteries of God's love and pardon will not be known in this life. The steadfastness of countless Christians is one indicator to the profit accruing from frequent Mass attendance. If the Mass is the "most holy and divine work" (Council of Trent, Sess.

22), it must be the most profitable and rewarding.

St. Paul was so enthralled by the thought of what divine grace does to the soul that he said, "When a man becomes a new creature in Christ, his old life has disappeared, everything has become new about him" (2 Cor. 5:17). Everything! Including his indigenous quitter's complex, his "will to fail," his fear of his infirmity. If it were not for the Mass, perhaps we would with Porcius Festus, think of Christ only as "a dead man called Jesus." But Christ lives on, making intercession for us in the Mass, that we might continue in the grace He won for us on the cross.

"That man will be saved, who endures to the last" (Mk. 13:13). And he can endure because the Mass remains, too, till the end of the world. The Mass remains, not alone in memory but in power (Denz. 938) "applied to the remission of those sins which we daily commit" (Deferrari, 288, 289). To keep on — it's a lofty goal. But man aspires to heights. Explorer I went to 200 miles minimum, the experimental rocket ship X-15 may rise to 150 miles, and a WAC Corporal rocket, mounted on a V-2, went 250 miles into the atmosphere. An air force rocket, launched from a high-altitude balloon rose nearly 4000 miles. The goal is high, but God generously has given means to attain it: one of the chief of these is the Mass. It is not surprising that faithfulness to duty goes with the Mass. The Mass is the unbloody sacrifice of the cross; the cross is the zenith of obedience to duty. Christ was obedient unto death, even the death of the cross. Father Alexander J. Cody, a priest of the Society of Jesus who died in 1958, was described by one of his friends as one who served faithfully. "Faithfulness," wrote Father Peter Newport, S.J., "is the keynote of Father Cody's character." At the close of his life Father Cody one day said to his friend with great sadness, "Peter, they won't let me offer holy Mass any more." Almost his last words were, "I must reach towards Eternal Love." In the Mass we not only reach but we take hold of and grasp that Love in our hands and in our hearts.

The Mass Around the World

"I often think," remarked a Josephite priest whose work in the deep South had been hard and demanding, "of little Bernadette Soubirous, elevating her thoughts to the Masses in the world, and even in her sickness uniting her soul with the greatest worship and love of God."

There have been theologians who argued that a person cannot profit from Masses at which he is not present; but they and their reasoning fall short of a saint's. And their reasoning may also fall short of common sense, because they will tell you that if a person wills to think of evil, wills to unite to evil-doing, that person is guilty of evil surely. If this is so, then the person who unites with good, and wills to unite with a good act such as the Mass, will get a reward for his acts of the will. If he unites with evil and shares the guilt of the specific sin, so also a person must be able to unite with good and share the reward of the specific good.

Bernadette delighted in offering to God the Masses going on all over the world; she was taking delight in the greatest good of all. Will her reward be less than that of a person who delights in a lesser good? The Holy Scripture has special reprobation for the man who "delights in iniquity," but a special reward too for the one who "rejoices in holiness." Such a one was Bernadette with her pious little picture of a clock face on which she read the hours at which Mass was being offered in every part of the earth, and her little print, pinned to the bed curtains, showing a priest elevating the Sacred Host. Sometimes the saint would call out to the little altar boy depicted there, "Now then, ring the bell!" "Her great happiness," Canon Perreau declared, "was to join in spirit in the holy sacrifices which, at that very moment, were being celebrated in this or that part of the world."[1]

With Bernadette we can follow the Mass around the world. Nearly half a million Masses are said each day in this wheeling globe as it hurries with perfect precision through a trackless gulf to its ultimate rendezvous with God.

6 o'clock: Christ begins His daily walk among the members of His family, in the heartland of America. St. Louis, perched on the muddy Mississippi, greets the King of kings, and Omaha, Kansas City, and Milwaukee acknowledge His presence.

In Antarctica, Father Daniel Linehan, S.J., seismologist-member of Operation Deepfreeze, stands on a predella of

[1] Francis Trochu, *Saint Bernadette Soubirous,* trans. and adapted by John Joyce, S.J. (New York, Pantheon Books Inc., 1957), p. 364.

glacial ice 3000 feet thick and offers the adorable sacrifice. In a subzero world populated by a few lean lichen and the eternal cold, the Source of life comes to warm the souls of scientists and sailors. A few hundred miles away, the South Pole, bottom of the world, lies bleak and icily aloof in the baleful half-light of the antarctic winter.

7 o'clock: Denver, Montreal, Mexico City — more stations on Christ's expedition to the hearts of humanity.

Behind the elaborately wrought stone lace work of the village *parrochia*, a Mexican priest lifts the spotless Host to God, while the people of Guanajato kneel on bare flagstones, brown arms outstretched. Bundles of dried peppers dangle from their rope belts, and their dusty sombreros lie on the benches. Chickens to be marketed that day lend their frenetic, cracked soprano to the awesome stillness. An Indian child kneels beside his mother, his round, inscrutable eyes mirroring the flickering candles, and shafts of solid sunlight knife from above and smash themselves to pieces on the baldachin, all in gold leaf, hovering over the main altar like the lid of a rich ciborium. In the plaza outside, wiry lads in peacock-colored finery dance and shoot off fire works to tell the town that Señor Jesucristo has come again.

8 o'clock. Next stop: Los Angeles, great growing center of the California Southland. In Point Loma, farther south, a party of fishermen attends Mass and Communion prior to a deep-sea fishing trip off the Coronado Islands. Spokane and Portland in the north are host to the Prince of Peace. Shipyard workers and stevedores kneel in worship before Him.

A religious at the main altar of the towering church of the Gesu in Milwaukee pronounces the sacred words before a quiet worshiping throng clad in storm coats and furs. Outside, sleety winds whine across Lake Michigan's shore, strewn with great, tilted shards of ice. Snow in wispy festoons trails off high gray gables and huddles in the corners of mullioned windows, gilded by the light within. Collegians look up from their prayer books and Missals as Jesus is raised above the heads of a craning world. "My Lord and my God."

In festive, sweltering Papua, a missionary lifts the small chalice of a military chaplain, containing the blood of Christ shed for his little flock. That flock includes a dozen native Fuyughé tribesmen gorgeous in cassowary feathers and jungle cosmetics, who kneel on a dirt floor before their Creator. Outside radioactive fall-out from atomic tests in the Pacific drifts down among the jungle trees.

9 a.m. Seattle, San Francisco, and British Columbia echo the divine footfall, as Christ tirelessly moves among this haggis of humanity.

A 76-year-old priest, kindly, wrinkled face etched with deep ruts, offers the Holy Sacrifice for the 21,251st time on his golden jubilee day. At the memento for the dead, his head drops; his eyes, swimming with tears, are fixed upon the precious Victim Host on the corporal before him. "Remember," he whispers in his heart, "good and loving Lord, all those who have gone on ahead: my mother and father, my friends. . . ."

10 o'clock. To Juneau and eastern Alaska the eternal High Priest brings the priceless thaw of His forgiveness and love. In a sod mission church He repeats the inexorable plea: "Forgive them, Father . . ."

An overflow crowd of business people crowds beautiful St. Peter's in the Chicago Loop. In that rich marble sanctuary, in the heart of the commercial center of one of the world's busiest cities, the Son of God goes about His business: the commerce of man with God. A Chinese seminarian on vacation for

the summer lifts his eyes to the Host and his heart drifts
back to Nanking, to a nut-oil factory, to his family dead now.
He makes his heart heard before Jesus.

11 o'clock, as the earth turns on its axis. And Christ bends
with pierced hands and side over the seaport cities of Welling-
ton and Auckland, New Zealand. Christ is at home everywhere. The Mass is at home everywhere.

Soapweed was blowing in the boisterous wind, across the
prairie, as the boy scouts knelt at their field Mass up in
Westminster, north of Denver. The father of one of the boys,
as he knelt, noticed the great tumble weeds rolling along,
bounding through the fields. In how many places the Mass is
offered! And always it is "in place." Hospital wards in the
army hospitals, dugouts, sick rooms, prison camps (Father Jim
Moynihan saying Mass twice a month in the new Denver
jail) — all these places are "proper" for the Mass because God
comes to His people wherever they are. Christ does not leave
them, not a single one, orphans.

In the frozen tundra above Siberia's arctic circle lies notori-
ous Vorkuta, Soviet slave-labor camp. There Jesuit Father
Pierre Leoni offered Mass in his cell in the bleak dawn of a
63-degree-latitude morning. His vestments were a small stole,
sewed by himself in moments stolen from back-breaking toil
in the coal mines. He prayed especially for his 80,000 fellow
slave laborers in Vorkuta! Into a chalice turned from a tiny
aluminum cylinder by a Hungarian prisoner Father Leoni
poured a few precious drops of wine. He had wheedled the
grapes from Communist guards. "My health demands it!" And
the spiritual health of how many other souls!

From these carefully hoarded dried grapes he squeezed some
juice, fermented it, stored the liquid treasure in a tiny perfume bottle. That wine and a few crumbs of bread became the

body and blood of Christ. Father Leoni read the Mass from the Missal of his memory, which the Communists had not yet confiscated. Standing at a box by his bunk, the bearded Jesuit said Mass while outside his cell two prison guards squatted to get out of the 60-below-zero wind roaring in off the tundra and spoke in guttural whispers of the people's republic and their aches and pains.

2 o'clock. The sacrifice of Christ sweeps across the face of the world, leaving the earth full of the grace of God, as David once wrote (Psalm 118), little dreaming of the fulfillment his words would find. Yap, the Caroline Islands, Truk, shimmering in the Pacific, battleground of World War II with memories of steaming carriers and flaming torpedo bombers, the sudden explosive light of flame throwers, and the four-engined crescendo of B-29's flinging themselves off hastily laid metal landing strips toward distant Nagasaki. Now the Prince of Peace comes, soothing the wounds, stanching the tears, silencing the moans, filling the emptiness with His Presence.

Ninety-year-old Father Eduardo Vitoria, S.J., devoutly offers his 20,000th Mass in Barcelona, Spain, in the presence of members of the Sarria Chemical Institute he founded 50 years before. "It's the greatest satisfaction of my life," he murmurs later, "offering more than 20,000 Masses!"

In a rural Wisconsin village prosperous wheat and dairy farmers gather in their church with their healthy children around them. Their pastor calmly offers the Holy Sacrifice for them in freedom from fear and want. In a nearby pasture placid Guernseys and Holsteins, heads deep in the rich, green grass, pause from grazing and lift their heads to the tinkle of Mass bells, tripping with crystal precision across the clover and alfalfa fields.

Father Anthony Bauer, Divine Word missionary Father, has

pedaled his bike torturous, steamy miles through the rolling bush country of Ghana on the East Coast of Africa from his mission station in Kwahu Tafo. Now he celebrates Mass in Suhum, and the God of riches descends into a church made entirely out of empty kerosene cases, lovingly fashioned by the natives. Two hundred black-skinned Christians have come to worship on the Feast of Corpus Christi. Outside, the chatter of monkeys and macaws tries to establish a beachhead of sound in the powerful stillness. Natives in worn khakis and flowery print dresses bow their heads and utter their heartfelt, "Lord, I am not worthy."

Only a whisper of wind is choir for a Mass offered by the chaplain of a boys' camp near Estes Park, Colorado, on an improvised altar atop the north peak of the Twin Sisters. The mountain arches more than 10,000 feet into the antiseptic blue of the dawn sky. Timberline lies far below, where scrub pines suddenly halt their slatternly advance and leave the peak crowned with a ragged tonsure. Heavy-booted climbers receive Communion. Across a chasm of blue sky, Longs Peak wakes from its slumber in a cascade of July sunshine.

Bishop André-Marie Charue, in quiet Namur, Belgium, presides at a Solemn Pontifical Mass, and the Cathedral choir chants the 1600-year-old Nicene Creed. In another key, Mrs. McGinity's quavering voice explores the *Dies Irae* in a small stone church off O'Connell Street, Dublin, with its bluster of traffic, all dominated by the great bronze statue of the famous statesman who gave the street its name. As that carven face looks out toward a bridge over the Liffey River, the Divine Statesman visits Dublin, not in bronze but in bread and wine, and departs again. And Dublin will never be the same.

3 o'clock. The Calvary Limited (bringing love unlimited) is right on schedule. Priests in Japan and Australia pour wine,

and their own intentions, into the chalice. "Place all your cares on the paten," Father Joseph Spae, C.I.C.M., tells his parishioners in Himeji, Japan, before he begins Mass. At 5 o'clock, uneasy Formosa is host to Christ. The rhythm of the Preface is punctuated by a salvo of gunfire erupting from the Red Chinese mainland.

Father Rawley Meyers, riding the circuit of the Nebraska missions in his dusty Ford, visits Winnebago, Tecumseh, Red Cloud, Fort Robinson, and Chimney Rock. The hum of horsepower over old Indian trails sends ring-necked pheasants and red-winged blackbirds clambering into the sky, splitting the morning quiet with whir of wing and sputter of crimson and gold. Then the wheat lands are still again where buffalo herds fell victim once to lean, raw-bitten cowboys under Buffalo Bill Cody. Standing over the fossil remains of some Mesozoic behemoth, Father Meyers changes bread and wine into Christ's living body and blood.

Only long hikes through roadless interiors brought the missionary to a remote *barrio* in the Philippines. He says Mass now, and the mutter of prayers in Tagalog filters up through the thatched roof and reaches even to the heart of God. In the parish of the Infant Jesus (*Tondo*) in Manila, the pastor in the memento for the living remembers his more than 86,000 parishioners!

Christ in the Mass moves on, bridging continents, following out the timetable of salvation: India and Ceylon at 7 o'clock, Iraq, Madagascar, and Ethiopia at 8.

A stone's throw from the gate of Ephraim in the old Jerusalem city wall stood a place of execution called Golgotha, hill of skulls (perhaps because of dead men's bones to be found there). It was here at 3 in the afternoon that Jesus died on the cross, with perfect resignation and willingness, for men.

Now our timetable reads 9 o'clock; Christ is back once more in Jerusalem, offering the same sacrifice He offered on the cross on Calvary, now without pain, with mystic death. A handful of humanity saw the pain, watched the life ooze from open wounds and fall, drop by drop, upon the grateful, receptive dust beneath. No blood flows now, but Christ's sacrifice is offered with the same power. And our hearts are dust, and into them comes the blood of Christ, the whole Christ, in Holy Communion.

Christ is on schedule. Syria and Turkey receive the King of kings. And at 10 o'clock the troubled Congo reverberates, not with booming of voodoo drums but with the silver thrum of Mass bells. Rhodesia and Greece and Egypt of the fabled pyramids stand in the spotlight of God's beneficence while Mass is offered, in many languages, in many Rites, but for all that the same sacrifice. It will save humanity yet, despite its stubborn nisus toward despair and disintegration.

Fifteen first graders in white satin and lace kneel in the front pew of their parish church in Moosup, Connecticut. Their hands are solemnly folded, rosary beads carefully entwined, and over the tips of spiring fingers round eyes peer toward the altar, source of life and love. In Denver, a choir of octogenarians and Little Sisters of the Poor chants a high Mass in an old people's home. One of the choir members is suspended on a pair of crutches, another is settled in a wheel chair. Their voices teeter over the notes of a Gregorian *Kyrie*, waveringly cling to a distropha, then tumble with gentle croaks down the steep edge of a tall clivis, only to rise again, like a tattered musical Phoenix from the ashes. It is the Feast of St. Joseph, and in that red sandstone home, in the scrubbed and gleaming chapel, the agony of notes dies out, while a few whispered words draw down the sum and substance of divinity into a tubercular priest's trembling hands and into a worn chalice.

Christ strides through the human race, gathering his children to Him in the embrace of the Mass. Time: 11 o'clock. Place: Rome, heart of Christendom, Germany, Sweden. Cast of characters: Jesus Christ, and the members of His Church. Action: the divine sacrifice of the Mass.

Lobster fishermen on the tip of South Africa know that the Mass insures them a "big catch" of God's grace. Sicilian and Portuguese fishermen, when the crawfish are running, hoist their rough red canvas sails and shove off; by nightfall they return with as many as 800 pounds of fish, and the water running high on the gunwhales. Mackerel and snoek clamber into their nets, and the poor flock to the beaches to have a feast on crawfish claws unwanted by the canneries. Thanks must be given to God who provides the fish and the good seasons. The Mass lifts the glad hearts of these fisher folk and says what they cannot say.

At 4:30 in the afternoon, in the chapel in an army hospital, Mass is offered. It resounds like an echo of the continual morning diapason of praise. And the timetable reads midnight. The Light of the world shines in France, Belgium, and England. Like a deep surf whose words roll in across the continents: "This is my body. This is the chalice of my blood."

A missionary among the eskimos, Mass kit packed securely in his dog sled, mushes through an ice field, across a frozen savannah, toward a lonely settlement in the merciless snowlands where he will say Mass on an altar of ice amid the igloos. There, his vestments stand out stiff in the cold over his fur parka, and in the distance, solemn penguins, standing like Fourth Degree Knights of Columbus, form a guard of honor for the greatest of all human events.

Four hundred haggard prisoners in Hanoi, North Vietnam, knelt in a square of barbed wire while Father Albert Stihle, French Redemptorist, said Mass. A drinking glass was chalice, a biscuit tin the ciborium. "It was my first Mass in 20 months," said the priest. He heard confessions for seven and one-half hours the previous day.

1 a.m. The homeless, itinerant Preacher of Galilee speaks again, in the words of the Mass offered at altars in Ireland, Portugal, Spain. Whole peoples cock an ear and tune their hearts to hear: And God said, Let there be light; and Jesus said, Let there be life.

In every crisis of life, in every mood and changing of the heart, the Mass is the stuff of strength for humans in the wrench and tug of circumstance. A widow and her six children kneel near the coffin of their husband and father, dead of a pulmonary embolism. Instinctively they turn to the Mass. The catafalque is somber in its black swathe of drape, and above at the high altar spangled with flickering candles the great Sacrifice goes on: a Sacrifice that takes its value in *death*, the death of Jesus. For the Mass is God's best guarantee of eternal life for us who are destined all to die.

Under the bruise-blue surface of the Mediterranean, the Holy Sacrifice is offered in the U. S. Navy submarine *Bang*, gliding peacefully in the marine semidarkness. As shadowy forms dart away in terror from the mightily humming intruder, *Bang* proceeds at ten knots, bearing its awesome, unearthly, beneficent Guest. Father Peter J. Ferreri, circuit-riding Navy chaplain, whispers the ancient prayers of the Canon aboard the Connecticut-based sub prying through the sea off the shores of Palestine. The Mass goes everywhere; everywhere the Mass is in place. All over the world, under the sea, and in the sky. A young boy once dreamed of being a flyer, but later turned his gaze deeper and he decided to make Christ his squadron commander. Christ was earthbound; when the devil tempted Him to fly off the temple roof, He spurned him, and flew instead into the hearts of men, and now flies around the world on the swift lips of priests at Mass. Now this boy is offering Mass in the spacious basket of a balloon, seven miles above the earth.

2 a.m. by the timetable. The Mass has swung down off the coast of South Africa to the Canary Islands, and sweeps across the South Atlantic past tiny, rock-ribbed Ascension Island, into Brazil.

In a grim Communist prison in Lishui, Chekiang, China, a curious guard peers in a peephole at his prisoner. Then he shoulders his gun and moves on, for the prisoner, Father Louis A. Venadam, Scarboro Foreign Mission priest, is only having breakfast. But it is a meal God Himself prepared. Father Venadam is saying Mass on a small box spread with a clean white shirt. He doesn't know where the bread and wine came from. One day, as a guard shuffled by in the corridor, a package thudded to the floor at his feet. It contained bread and wine. Three days later, "mystery" bread and wine become the "mystery of faith," the body and blood of Christ, while a guard glances in, scuffs his shoes, and moves on, satisfied his prisoner is taking his breakfast.

3 o'clock. Next stop: Argentina, British Guiana. The tireless Jesus immersed Himself in our flesh, our world, our time, our space — and again and again in our bread and our wine. What does wheat have to look forward to? A hard harvesting, journey to a mill, punishment that makes it flour. Then mixture with water, then death and the tomb of the oven, from which it emerges triumphantly as bread. And if that bread becomes the body and blood of Christ! *That* is what bread looks for-

ward to. Grapes look beyond the busy hands of vineyard workers, the agony of the Garolla Crusher, burial in the fermentation vat; beyond the dinner parties, toasts, nightcaps, and see as their great goal: to become Christ's body and blood. "The whole of nature," St. Paul said, "as we know, groans in a common travail all the while" (Rom. 8:22). Why? In anticipation of a spiritual harvest. God has made humans His adopted children, bread and wine have become His Son's flesh and blood. All creation groans for *this:* intimacy with God. The Mass more than anything else in the world makes that hope of all the ages unprecedented reality.

Ecuador, Chile, and Nova Scotia are our next stops, as the timetable says 4 a.m.

A cardinal of the Church offers a canonization Mass in St. Peter's in Rome, with the Holy Father in his white splendor presiding. Eighty thousand worshipers kneel in the presence of Christ, the sanctuary is afire with prelatial crimsons. Outside, where a vast painting, depicting the new saint, streams from a high balcony, 200,000 people rock the great square with their acclamations.

Skiers in gay parkas and sweaters kneel in a prefab chapel and hear Mass. Up above, along the cool and brilliant slopes of Berthoud Pass in the Rockies, shadows seem to schluss and slalom when the wind rocks the pines and gnarled spruce. The sun comes up gently around a cornice of stone, and the priest reads the Gospel: And Christ said, "Thou art Peter, and on this rock . . ." In Albuquerque, in a gusty April morning, a mother sits quietly meditating on the mysteries of the Mass. In her lap, her infant contentedly takes his bottle.

Technicians lay aside geiger counters and tools and kneel on the barren Nevada desert as a tanned priest offers Mass on the back of a jeep. In the background a steel tower stands gauntly. In a few days an atomic bomb will be exploded from its shed-like summit. Now technicians, scientists, army engineers, security guards, and reporters kneel in a scraggly growth of pinyon pines and pray for peace.

The Mass does go almost everywhere. Early in 1958 Father Frederick Trumbull offered Mass in front of a cave 17,000 feet up Africa's Mount Kilimanjaro. Leader of the geological survey, John Tunstall of Johannesburg, South Africa, asked the Bridgeport, Conn., priest to join the safari so that daily Mass might be offered. The Mass is offered, too, to celebrate great occasions in the lives of men and women. The priest has always accompanied his people in the events of their daily lives. When the Kammon undersea tunnel, linking Honshu with Kyushu, was opened in the spring of 1958, the lead car in the procession of vehicles to make the first trip carried a Shinto priest to "purify the way."

When Frau Elizabeth Reindl of Rochusfeld, Germany, observed her 101st birthday in 1958, she marked the day by attending Mass. She said she had been going to daily Mass ever since she could remember. When the Irish hunt season was opened at Kilfeacle, for members of the Kilfeacle Beagle Hunt Club, the Mass of St. Hubert was offered in St. Patrick's Church. St. Hubert is the patron saint of huntsmen.

Savage Xavantes Indians from the interior of Brazil crowd around the bearded Salesian as he offers Mass. Since 1910, Father Anthony Colbacchini, now past 70, has had this as his goal: to offer Mass in the midst of, as well as for the intentions of, his beloved Xavantes. In 1934, two Salesian missioners went into this wilderness of vines and violence to bring the tender pity of Christ to the "savages of Lagoa." Their bodies lie somewhere in that exotic earth, near the spot where they were poleaxed by Xavantes tribesmen.

As Father Colbacchini reads the Epistle, naked children squat at his heels and tug at his chasuble. A child in his mother's arms reaches out with a tiny hand and pulls at his beard. Some of the savages run their dark fingers along the pages of the Missal. Two of the men, Ereboanan and Jurura, remember other priests of the Salesians. That was in 1934, and they had left those two ambassadors of Christ lying in pools of their own blood on the jungle floor. Now they look on curiously as God's greatest gift to man goes on before them. Afterward, white settlers and Xavantes dine on deer and wild hog, while westward Christ continues to offer Himself to the Father by the lips and hands of His priests.

Manhattan rises over the horizon, as the Mass goes round the world. The timetable says 5 a.m. Cuba, Honduras, and Jamaica pour their prayers into the pierced palms of our Lord, and He lifts them up, higher than the Empire State Building, up above the traffic patterns where airliners and military jets wheel and whiz, so high that the Father can hear them, our prayers.

Deep in the Maine woods a priest-scientist offers Mass on a portable altar placed carefully among ferns and pines. An inquisitive chipmunk, perched on stacks of seismological equipment, works at a husk of walnut, then scampers out of sight among a clump of boulders as the tinkle of a bell tells of the approach of the Bread of Heaven to appease the world's hunger. And down in Honduras, workers for banana and chicle growers cluster round an adobe hut where Mass is being celebrated by a young missionary, clad in khaki, boots muddied by a tropical cloudburst. As he genuflects before the God of Purity, a khaki pants leg lavishly anointed with mud shows for a moment under the wrinkled alb. His mouse-colored donkey, tethered to a shrub, browses contentedly, skin still glistening from the morning downpour. TV cameras focus on a score of young men prostrate on the marble floor of St. Patrick's Cathedral in New York City.

6 o'clock by the timetable and Christ has completed His tour of His people, and back in St. Louis, in the Old Cathedral with its gold mosaics, a young priest makes the sign of the cross and says, *"Et introibo ad altare Dei."* Once more Jesus begins His ceaseless visitation of all His people. The world is His parish; He never leaves it but daily works in it, perhaps in the luxurious chapel of an ocean-going liner bound for Southampton; or in Kalgoorlie, Australia; in a prefabricated chapel for workers in the Saudi Arabian oil fields; in the air-conditioned chapel of a hospital in Cleveland; on a makeshift altar in the shadow of a British tank near Madras, India, with an oil-stained tarp as baldachin. The "priest-worker" movement is a delicate one; many difficulties arose in connection with it. But one of the interesting facets of the movement is that it was stopped, or rather modified, for other reasons and *not* that the Mass was "out of place" in the factory or tenement or shop. The Mass belongs to man, and is found wherever man is found.

What is the "proper setting" for the Mass? Is it only an ornate monastery altar, or an elaborate Cathedral altar of Carrara marble with its golden canopy? My cowpoke friend Zeb Trierweiler, once remarked, "Some folks think of Mass bein' said in the jungle or some rambledown shack as bein' jist not proper, and as sorter an excuse for what it orter be. But that ain't exackly so, cuz there is sompin' pritty proper to my way o' thinkin' in havin' Mass the way it allus wuz meant to be, jist close to the people. There's sumpin' awful homey to me when I wuz at the Masses we used to say from the hind end of a jeep, and the boys wuz all sittin' aroun' prayin' their hearts out jist to keep alive over there. And evvah time we heard a drone we knew it could jist uz well be some blasted Kamikaze reddy to dive on the hul bunch of us an' blast us to kingdom cum. I thought plenty times whut a lot of concentrated prayer I sed them days!

"'N the priest wuz sometimes so skinny that I figured he'd been on rations fer weeks, we mebbe wuz havin' trouble gettin' rations through. Talk about fastin' and morteefykashun! There was plenty of it, and I reckon the monks had nothin' on us fer keepin' the holy season.

"Plenty of times there wuz a Requiem for sevril at one time, with only a few bits of the bodies of the boys that'd been blown up by some bomb. And we'd pick up a bit here and a bit there and count how many wuz left, and only then know how many there had been, and how many the Funril Mass was bein' sed fer. And the padre would sing 'Rekwieskat in pachee' and those of us as wuz left'd sing an 'Aymen.' There wuzn't no make believe, then, 'n we didn't have no fancy coffin.

"Sometimes, I recollect how the padre wuz off key, and didn't allus sing the right notes. Course, I'm no Crewso. Anyhoo, the Mass belonged there jist as much, 'n mebbe more. Them poor boys thet wuz blasted into eternity needed it, cuz they didn't have no time fer much more 'n a general absolution by the padre's quick 'absolvo te' — but he switched to 'absolvo vos' when he heerd them suicide planes whinin' in. I knew a little Latin from the days when I was a shaver 'n the sisters made me study. 'N I recollect too thet at the same Mass thet we wuz burryin' what wuz left of the others, the padre give us Communion, only he called it Viaticum."

Around the world with the Mass — in 24 hours, every day of the year. Mass and people go together. The times our Lord said Mass, as far as we know, there was no elaborate setting: once in a hired upper room, another time in a roadside inn for overnight stops at Emmaus.

"I go along," Zeb Trierweiler concluded, knocking some pasture mud off his cowboy boots, "thet everythin' orter be done to make the Mass be in a right byooteeful settin'. But it ain't out of place in an old 'dobe hut, like we have out on the mesa, where the Mexican padre says Mass fer us boys at roundup time, with the cryin' of the dogees and bawlin' of the restless cattle cumin' in through the cracks in the walls. I figger that if people are there, it's right fittin' fer the Mass to be there, too."

Mankind Needs the Priest

WHEN God made man from the dust of the earth and breathed into his face His living image, He left in man a devouring need: the need for Himself. With that need went the obligation of paying some kind of recognition to it. A child was once asked why it threw itself into its father's arms each evening when he returned from work. "Because he's my daddy," was the reply. We worship God because He *is* God. Just by existing we pay some tribute to the Intelligence that subsidizes us. But God wants more than that. Since we are intelligent and free, He wants a love that is intelligent and free.

Man's beliefs in God express themselves in his actions and in his efforts to acknowledge that Supreme Something Else or Someone Else. His religious acts, such as sacrifice, are outshinings of his inward, abstract creed. The creed (or formulary of beliefs) demands a certain set of actions and forbids others (code). The acts of worship are called cult. These are the "CCC element" of every religion: creed, code, cult. They form the complexus of relationships binding man to God and called "religion."

At the head of a people worshiping God there has marched at every step of the world's way a priest. He has been the official representative of the people with God, deputed to stand for all the rest in publicly offering acts of worship to the Almighty. Religion has always had its priests.

Greek, Roman, Tocharian, Hittite, Sumerian, Etruscan civilizations had each its legally deputed envoys from mankind to God. Official traffic in prayer and adoration has been carried on historically in the name of the multitude by a duly appointed corps of hieratic diplomats, the priests. Just such a representative was the Mayan high priest of the Chacs, insatiable rain gods, as he wielded his flint knife on some luckless Zoque slave; so too the turbaned medicine man in Madhya Pradesh, central India, officiating at a banquet of roasted fellow tribesmen in some grim jungle sanctuary; and the priest of the Greek goddess Artemis, smashing a pot of expensive oil against a wall of her temple at Perakora near Corinth as a plea for good sailing. Each of the pueblos of the American Indians, descendants of the Anasazi ("ancient ones" in Navajo), has its Cacique (kuh-see-kee), who is in charge of all religious activities.

Not just any citizen can present himself in an official capacity before the government of the United States or the court of a king. He must first have credentials which establish him as an official representative of his nation. Without this portfolio he is not recognized. Not just any citizen can represent mankind before God to offer sacrifice, adore, thank, propitiate, and ask favors. This function demands a legitimate functionary, an ordained emissary from the human race. Only such an emissary is admitted to the office of priest; the ordination makes him such a representative.

The priest is designed with sacrifice in view. Without sacrifice, there is no priesthood. Hence Protestants have ministers or preachers, but not priests, since they have no sacrifice.

The priest *belongs*. He is an integral part of society. He is not out of place, not something added over and above what is required. The priest is a necessity. Why? Because the world cannot get along without the Mass, and only the priest can offer Mass. John C. H. Wu, noted Chinese jurist, once declared, "I view the priesthood as such a sacred vocation that even in writing to my own son who is still in the seminary, I often sign myself as 'Your potential altar-boy.' "[1]

The world must pay its debt of worship to God. There are no such things as time payments in God's economy of grace: the Mass pays off that debt of worship in a lump sum, and the human debtor makes his own the adoration of the Mass by frequent attendance. "The entire Church," said St. Alphonsus Liguori, "cannot give to God as much honor, nor obtain so many graces as one priest saying one Mass." In the Mass Christ, God's divine Son, is both offerer and offered, both sacrificed and sacrificing, both priest and victim. He functions in the Mass (as on the cross) in His official capacity as head or high priest of humanity. Christ in the Mass officially and

---

[1] From an address delivered at the Second World Congress of the Lay Apostolate held in Rome in 1958.

publicly represents to God the Father all the needs of His Church and of each of its members. His work (the Mass) shares in His personal dignity which is infinite.

If the function, the Mass, is a must, so too is the functionary, the priest. There is no Mass without the priest. Not that he is the primary player in the divine drama. That role is reserved for Jesus. "The priesthood is not . . . something," Cardinal Suhard wrote, "it is *someone*: Christ." Or in the words of the Curé of Ars, "The priesthood is the love of the Heart of Jesus" for mankind, a love perpetually enshrined in the Mass. And it is not just enshrined there, like a Sumerian dishpan in a museum; rather it is active in the Mass, working, pleading, getting results, saving souls. It is very evidently due to Masses said daily throughout the world that martyrs are granted their constancy in persecution, the laity their meritorious fidelity to their duties, nuns their heroism in their labors for Christ, priests their devotion to His life cause, the good of men. The priesthood is Christ's priestly (sacrificing, forgiving, teaching) power incarnate in a human being. Thus Cardinal Suhard's "The priesthood is Christ."

The priest in the Mass, like Christ, *must* act as the ambassador of humanity, not in his personal capacity as a private citizen. No Mass, then, can really be a private Mass because no priest can say Mass in his own name, as a private citizen. To the extent he is a private person, he is incapable of saying Mass. He must be acting as the public representative of mankind. Circumstances of privacy (viz., the "hidden" Mass of the Camaldolese monk in a distant cloister attended only by the altar boy) cannot invade the solemn act of worship of the High Priest, acting through His earthly representative, the priest. This is so because of the Mass's public character, as official act of the chief of all men. The Mass of its very nature is offered for all mankind, just as was its prototype, the sacrifice of the cross, identical with the Mass in all but mode or manner.

How does the priest, who holds his commission from God, function as artist of human salvation? What is his role at his atelier, the altar of God? He is the instrumental cause by his human acts, filling the role of the brush in painting, the typewriter in writing, the transit in surveying. Through the priest's instrumentality, bread and wine become the body and blood of Jesus; through him *something* becomes *Someone.* The paintbrush in the grasp of a Jean Ingres or John Marin is an irrational instrument. The priest, in the grip of God, is in the Mass a rational instrumental cause. His instrumentality is through his will. He freely co-operates, marshaling his intelligence and will to blend with the action of Christ in the consecration. It is not merely the priest's words which effect the transubstantiation of bread and wine. It is his *willed* words. The words of consecration (*Hoc est enim corpus meum, Hic est enim calix sanguinis mei* . . .) are full of the will of the priest. A tape recording of the words of consecration would not affect the bread and wine, no matter how often the recording was played. For such words are empty words, empty of the life-giving spirit of priestly understanding and consent. Such words lack efficacy precisely because they lack the will of an ordained ambassador of God.

A document has little or no value if it lacks the will (intention) of the signer. On March 28, 1945, 16 members of the Polish underground government went to dine with Communist Marshal Zhukov, ostensibly to map out future Russo-Polish relations. Actually the 16 were clapped into Lubianka prison for "interrogation." The betrayal was followed by grillings of from three to fifteen hours, with a blinding light shining in their faces, constantly interrupted sleep, little food. Fifteen of them "confessed" their guilt of conspiring with the Germans against the Red army then fighting in Poland. Only one, a lawyer named Stypulkowski, failed to crack. Yet of what value were the "confessions" of the other fifteen? Their signatures lacked will or intention. Their will was coerced. Robert A. Vogeler, assistant vice-president of the International Telephone and Telegraph Company, was arrested on false espionage charges by the Hungarian Reds in Budapest on November 18, 1949. Until April 28, 1951, when he was finally released, Vogeler endured the most exquisite torture. For the first 78 hours he was denied sleep, and finally collapsed while the brutal Communist interrogators waved the phony confession under his nose. Through 18-hour daily grilling, often under glaring lights, Vogeler lost the will to resist and at last signed the confession. On February 21, 1950, he was convicted and sentenced to 15 years in prison. The U. S. State Department later obtained his release by making diplomatic concessions to Hungary.

In the case of the Polish patriots and of Vogeler, the signatures meant nothing because the will or intention of the signer was not contained in them. The words of consecration must for the same reason be impregnated with the priest's will and intention to consecrate. Hence the Church, when pointing out the "form" of the sacrament of the Eucharist, namely, the words of consecration, adds another element: "and the faithful intention" (Denz. 424), or "with the intention of effecting" (Denz. 715). Words + intention = Body and Blood of Christ. Not just the words, not just the intention; but both, spoken by a duly ordained priest over wheaten bread and the fermented wine of the grape.

The priest may be looked at in two ways: as a natural

offerer and as a supernatural offerer. As a natural offerer he is in a sense a spiritual descendant of the ancient pagan priests who made sacrifices to God on behalf of their constituents (though their "god" was often an imperfectly apprehended deity or deities).

The method of choosing priests has varied. The head of Yucatan's religious hierarchy, Ah Kin Mai, inherited his priesthood from his father and passed it on in turn to his son. Priests were chosen from the sons of the Tzotzil Maya of Chiapas, from the tribe of Levi among the Jews. The "pontifices" or pontiffs (bridge builders), priests of early Rome, were self-elective till 104 B.C.; they chose members to suit their own requirements, and then only from the upper or patrician class till 300 B.C.

But the point is there were always priests (sometimes priestesses too) to carry out ritual worship of God in the name of the people. Everybody could not "get into the act." So certain individuals were selected to carry out the ceremonial. Ritual was formulated and fixed, then preserved in pious pandects for future generations of Mithraists, Isis cultists, Boutadae or ox-men (priests of Zeus and Athene), the Sarii or leaping priests of Mars, and what have you. Today's priest has a kinship with these countless pagan religious officials who carried out their punctilious ritual age after age in an effort to honor and placate the gods.

The ritual of the pagans and of the Jews, too, was almost purely ceremonial. Only the intention of the officiating priest and assisting people gave it a religious value. In pagan Rome, if the priest made the slightest mistake in rubrics, he had to repeat the whole ceremony — hardly a surprise when we reflect that in such a ritual sacrifice the ceremony was everything. In the Mass it is the consecration which is everything, the changing of bread and wine into the whole Christ, and not just the ritual activity. (A reminder, this, for priests who are *excessively* anxious about all the punctilios of the liturgy.)

Fixation on the ceremonial led inevitably to a kind of febrile scrupulosity over prayers and rites. The old Roman prayer to Mars during the ritual purification (lustration) of a field illustrates this scrupulosity. In it the pious Roman asks Mars to stop storms from taking place; or anyhow to keep them from coming near his own property; or at least to turn them back at the edge of his property if they do come near!

Father Martindale, S.J., has noted plays upon words in the Canon of the Mass which bear a similarity to this Roman preoccupation with all the aspects of a thing. E.g., *dona, munera, sacrificia* or *ratam, rationabilem, acceptabilem.*[2] There is, however, a profound difference between the prayers of the Mass and those of the pagan ritual, despite verbal similarities. In the pagan's search for nicety of phrase, for the right formula, is reflected his anxious, blind groping for a means of appeasing the gods. The Mass prayers, on the other hand, express the Christian's calm, uncontested possession of the perfect way of adoring God. The slightest nuances in verbs and adjectives used in the Mass are but a hopelessly weak insinuation of the Mass's infinite capacity for paying humanity's debt to God. The old Roman's solicitude for semantics in prayer is a confession of uncertainty and longing. Though he didn't know it, he was longing for the Mass.

The priest according to the order of Melchisedech operates on a level which is out of sight of the strange, curious, terrifying pagan ritual. His credentials are conferred by God via the sacrament of orders; they, permanently marking and em-

[2] C. C. Martindale, S.J., *Religions of Early Rome* (London: Catholic Truth Society).

107

powering his soul, outfit him for the colossal task of offering holy Mass. The Mass is no gallimaufry of ritual movements and murmurings, but the action of Christ (His mystical death) incarnate in the Consecration ritual, and in the priest celebrating.

"How can Christ die in the Mass, when the Bible says[3] that He is always *living* to make intercession for man?" asked a member of an instruction class in a St. Cloud, Minn., parish. Christ cannot die physically, with an actual separation of body from blood, such as took place on the cross. He dies sacramentally or mystically. When we deal with sacraments, we deal with signs. A signpost is a visible (or audible or sensible) clue to the existence of some state of affairs not seen. A road sign tells of a winding highway ahead, as yet out of sight behind an undulant ridge. A green signal light beside the mainline tells a locomotive engineer that the section ahead is clear.

The signs in each case tell us of some state of affairs beyond our ken. The sacraments are signs. They, like the highway sign and the signal light, tell us of something that lies beyond our purview. Baptism has for sign the pouring of water and the pronouncing of meaningful words, "I baptize you in the name of the Father . . ." What we can't see or measure is the change baptism works in the soul. The water is a sign of washing clean. That is what is happening in the soul of the person baptized. Here, of course, the sacraments part company with the road signs and the railroad signals. These latter only inform, without causing. The sacramental signs not only inform but also cause. Extreme Unction not only sym-

---

[3] Apoc. 5:1–7: Christ is there described as a lamb *stantem tamquam occisum*, "standing although slain." This is the paradoxical role of Jesus on the cross and in the Mass.

bolizes (informs us of) a strengthening but actually causes that strengthening in the soul of the sick person.

The Mass is similar to the sacraments. It has signs which not only inform but cause. What are these signs? They are the two consecrations. The first expresses the state of affairs: this (thing) is the body of Christ. The words, then, and the will of the priest change the whole substance of bread into Christ's body. Not His blood or divinity but His body alone. However, because Christ's body is everywhere as it is in heaven (knit into a unity with the blood, soul, and divinity), it must be on the altar in the same way. So by force of concomitance, as the theologian says, the blood and soul and divinity of Christ are present on the altar. But by force of the words, only the body is there. Similarly, the wine is changed into Christ's blood by force of the words, with body, soul, and divinity being present by force of concomitance (or accompaniment). So, by virtue of the priest's words, body and blood of Christ are separate; by concomitance, they are united. But in the Mass, as in the sacraments, the sign not only symbolizes but causes a hidden reality. Hence, body and blood of Christ are really separate, not in the historical order (as on Calvary), nor in the world of imagination. But really, and sacramentally.[4]

Historically, the sacrifice of Jesus is over and done with. The blood He shed is shed and the crosses have been taken down, the guards gone away, the people returned to their homes — but the world has been irrevocably changed. In the sacramental (and very real) order of things, that sacrifice continues in the Mass. It is not surprising that there should be

---

[4] This doctrine is set forth by the Council of Trent in Session XIII (Oct. 11, 1551), chapter 3, Denzinger 876. Cf. *The Sources of Catholic Dogma* (already referred to), trans. by Roy Deferrari (St. Louis: B. Herder Co., 1957), p. 267. See also the encyclical *Humani Generis*, 70: "Now the Eucharistic species under which He [Christ] is present symbolize the actual separation of His Body and Blood" (New York: Paulist Press).

blood connected with our salvation. On the Island of Malta, the Maltese people have a saying *"Ma ghandix demm mihau"* — I have no blood with him. It means, "I don't get along with him." If a man does have blood with another, there is a state of friendship established. Christ "has blood with us," having drawn His blood from His Mother, shed it on the cross, and poured it into our hearts in every Communion.

Sacrifice in itself, Father McKenzie has pointed out, "symbolizes man's belief in a community of exchange between himself and the deity."[5] The Breviary exclaims on the Octave day of the Nativity (Jan. 1) *O admirabile commercium* in describing the Incarnation. *Commercium* means "trade, commerce, communication," among other things, as well as "negotiations as to the ransom of prisoners." There is the precedent of the Church for speaking of God's dealings with man in terms of high finance and trade.

Christ had in mind the rejuvenation of the human race when He entered into it by becoming man (*commercium*). But mankind did not go along with His ethical preachings, though these held out the promise of genuine happiness and achievement. Instead, man longed for the fleshpots of autonomy and license, and put Jesus to death in its pellmell rush. Jesus was in the way. In the very crucifixion, the human race accomplished its redemption. Its crime, by divine irony, backfired, and that sharp roar (the roar of a temple curtain torn, of a shaken earth and opening tombs) concealed the triumphant orchestration of redemption.

When financier Hanns Ditisheim bought 100,000 shares of White Motor Co. stock at $13 a share, he had in mind

---

[5] John L. McKenzie, S.J., *The Two-Edged Sword* (Milwaukee, Wis.: The Bruce Publishing Co., 1956, second printing 1957), p. 125. This book, perhaps the best on the subject yet written, should be read in its entirety.

to revamp the company completely. His proposals were rejected and the company squeezed him out. Ditisheim sold his stock, but his maneuvers had brought its price to $48 a share, and he toted up a profit in the millions.

Jesus bought stock in the human race by becoming man. This incarnation has increased the value of mankind. The proposals Christ made for the reorganization of humanity were simple and severe: "love the Lord thy God" — "take up your cross" — "unless you be as little children" — "go and sin no more" — "blessed are the meek" — "keep watch, praying at all times." But those to whom Christ spoke in large part vetoed His proposals.

Christ, too, was squeezed out literally, His life oozing down the rough, wooden shank of a Roman cross. But in dying He brought the market value of mankind to its highest peak, for now the human soul was worth the life of the Son of God. Christ did not benefit from His death, since He is God and lacks nothing. But the human race benefited, despite its graceless rejection of His bid at reorganization. So the liturgy calls Adam's sin "felix culpa." Thus can all mistakes be termed, most of all the mistake of those who thought Jesus was possessed by the devil, and murdered the (to them) doctrinaire energumen. Thus they released the insupportable force of divine energy from His precious Body. It nourishes us to this day, nourishes us in the Mass.

Sacrifice, as Father McKenzie said, appeals most to simple, unsophisticated people. "Unless you become as little children . . ." A missionary in Alaska once wrote that there is much simplicity "out here on the frontier where the coils and complications of 'culture' haven't had time to wind. One finds that the difficulties slowly but surely whittle away at notions formerly held as sacred and supreme. In the end, I suppose

111

one would truly possess the core and unsullied essence of reality. One of the great obstacles up here is to battle with the state of continual confusion that comes with a completely new area, a completely new life . . . there is no tradition — and tradition is a power and a beauty. Never before have I felt the force and influence of sin on man's endeavor and works so much. We are so incapable of the least things. We are tiny, darkened, blinded beings groping to see a few inches ahead. The patterns of civilization and tradition provide society with at least a short view into the future. Up here in Alaska society is yet in the state of *fiendi* (becoming). This situation caters especially to patience and trust. It is a wonderful challenge to the formation of virtue. It continually exercises the mind, and the soul. And in it I have recourse to the Mass for the patterns, the tradition, the force for good I need and find lacking in myself and my environment. The Mass is my answer, and the answer of my simple people, to the demands of a simple, uncomplicated, terribly demanding life. I think I should die of loneliness and frustration, except for the Mass."

Man has usually put holy things such as sacrifice to God in the hands of a group set apart and designated as priests. It is not surprising that Catholics speak of the priest as "Father." A religious order priest related that on visiting his brother and his family, he noted how proud he and his wife were of their children — and rightly too, because they were handsome, intelligent, healthy youngsters. "One thought came vividly to me from observing them: how strong the affection and love and how completely unselfish the devotion of the parents. There was no amount of sacrifice that they would not go through for their children.

"Perhaps they can serve as a model for priests in priests' relation to God, who puts Himself in the relation of such close association with us. In a sense, the priest is the origin of God-incarnate-and-by-circumincession-the-Three-Persons-of-the-Trinity, when the priest consecrates. In a sense, the priest brings about the new birth of God-(incarnate-etc.) on the altar, because in the Mass Christ is 'born again.' It seems almost as though God wished to exploit every relationship of love in His devising means to be 'all things' to men, and arranged that man (the priest) should be, in a certain sense, the origin of God-(etc.).

"The priest bends slightly over the bread and wine, as the mother bends over the baby. The priest looks down into the chalice and sees his own reflected features in the sacred Cup of Wine that is God (in liquid form), somewhat the same as a man looks at the face of his son, and into his eyes that are so completely like his own. The father is the origin of his son, and the priest by his will and his words is the origin of God-incarnate-(etc.). Before his words and his act of the will, it was bread, now it is not; it was wine before, now it is more. . . .

"What complete and unselfish love parents have when they look into their children's eyes! Priests participate more in Christ's work of remaining with and redeeming men through the Eucharist; hence they look on the Eucharist with the same or more love and unselfish devotion than parents look on their children."

Hence the priest's love of the Mass. Father Robert J. Gray of Pittsburgh offers the Holy Sacrifice each morning from a wheel chair in his mother's home, while she and a sister recite the responses. He is happy to be able to fulfill the central purpose of his priesthood. A young priest in Cincinnati remarked: "When I say Mass, I feel that *this* is the whole reason for my existence as a priest." And yet the Mass is not the private domain of the priest. It belongs to all the people, "of whatever office or pre-eminence they are, as many as wish . . . to foster within themselves that life of divine grace, whose final end is the attainment of the blessed life with God."[6]

The Mass belonged to the people from the very beginning. In the early centuries, the people gathered in private dwellings for services and the "breaking of bread." The catacombs only rarely served as sites for the offering of Mass. Later on Mass was offered occasionally on the tombs of the martyrs, especially on the anniversary of their death. That was the exception to the rule.[7] The home housed the Mass then.

The entire life of Christ looked to the sacrifice He made on Calvary and took its whole effectiveness from the cross. The entire life of the priest, who acts in the person of Christ, looks to its own axis which is the re-enactment of Calvary, the Mass. There is no "as if" to the Mass. The Mass is not play acting. It is really the unbloody sacrifice of the cross. Everything in it points to its identification with Calvary. The sign of the cross, for instance. It is painted, embroidered, carved, sewed, embossed, printed, cast, stamped, and woven into the Mass as a bold reminder: *here* is where Jesus offers Himself for humanity. During the Mass the priest makes the sign of the cross 45 times, 29 of them over the offering. Five crosses are engraved on the altar stone, and in consecrating the altar the Bishop made the sign of the cross more than 100 times.

---

[6] Denz. 1978, *Sources of Catholic Dogma, op. cit.,* Herder, Deferrari translation, p. 502.

[7] The term *catacomb* is a place name for *one* of many Roman cemeteries, and was used as we use "Arlington" or "Forest Lawn." Other cemeteries in Rome were "Cucumber Hill Cemetery" and "Cemetery at the Capped Bear." Rome went underground seeking burial plots because of the large areas of dark, soft tufa forming much of the subsoil around Rome and, perhaps, to conserve real estate sites above ground. Even the most spacious of these underground rooms could not hold the large congregations of the time, and of course the cemeteries were too well known to the police. More safety was to be found in private homes.

On his back, as he ascends the altar, the priest carries a cross woven on his chasuble.

This is outward evidence of the inner reality. By faith we make contact with that reality. In the range of radiation of the electromagnetic spectrum, from cosmic rays measuring one trillionth of a centimeter to radio rays too long to be measured, the human eye is sensitive only to a slender band of light. Radiation outside this band is invisible to us. But if the eye could somehow be sensitized to rays a few hundred thousandths of a centimeter longer or shorter, the world would take on a frighteningly new and garishly strange face. Yet it would be the same world.

By faith we are sensitized to a whole new world of truths, to a new view of reality otherwise inaccessible to human understanding and belief: namely, that Christ operates in our midst, paying in the Mass all our debts to God. It is the same world without faith, but then the most critical values soar out of sight of humanity's myopic stare. Jesus is immolated in the Mass ("immolate" means to devote to death, to slay), in an unbloody, painless manner, for the good of the world. Faith attunes us to that fact, enables us to profit from it.

No substitute can be found for the Mass. It is unique. On February 13, 1956, Eugene Ormandy bowed into the cresting waves of applause from a capacity audience at the Academy of Music in Philadelphia. Then stepping smartly to the podium he raised his baton, brought it down, and through the hall resounded the opening chords of Paul Creston's "Fanfare for Brass." All at once Maestro Ormandy stopped conducting and lowered his baton. One by one the musicians laid down their instruments. But the music thundered on! As the audience stirred and whispered its unbelief, a concert official went up on the stage and explained that from the beginning the musi-

115

cians had not played a note. The whole performance had been a high fidelity recording!

No amount of fidelity, however high, can replace the Mass or substitute for it. Not private prayers or novenas or the lighting of candles, no processions or visits or music. A Navy chaplain stated the conclusion that should follow from these facts: "It isn't a question of, Can we afford to go to Mass? It's a question of, Can we afford to miss it?"

Priests draw pertinent meditations from the knowledge that they officially represent mankind. A senator does not write insulting letters to his constituents, nor belittle and pull to pieces those he represents. By the very fact he was chosen to represent their interests, he is as a senator presumed to have their good at heart. The priest, similarly, should never be harsh or uncharitable to his constituents. His constituents are all members of the human race. The priesthood is one of prevailing gentleness and joy. "Rejoice, again I say rejoice," advised St. Paul. Ranting pessimism and raving are out of place.

It is important to think of the priesthood in this grand style, as the office of liaison between God and man. Not as a mere means of pleasing Aunt Kate or of solving social or economic problems. Priests and seminarians recognize that they are assuming a full-time office, one mankind must fill if it would present its love, adoration, thanks, and requests to almighty God.

When the Japanese arrange a bowl of flowers, the whole ensemble of leaves, vase, stem, and flowers is considered. The leaves are usually thinned out to give "accent." The stems are often joined together in a tight bundle as if to form one stalk, especially if the vase is tall. The classical styles of arrangement always observe three levels, viz., *Chi* or earth, *Jin* or man, and *Ten* or heaven. The curves of stem and flowers are harmonious and restful to the eye. The direction of the curves is to the points of the compass, and the general effect is to fascinate the mind by producing with foliage, vase, and blossoms something like a geometer's compound curve.

The Mass operates on the highest level of all, that of the supernatural life of man. Man has vegetable, sentient, rational life, and most important a supernatural life in union with God by grace. Here the Mass works its greatest effects, solving the dissatisfaction of man wounded by sin and clawing his way toward intimacy with God. "There is no hope for the satisfied man," proclaims the masthead of the *Denver Post*. Yes, commented a priest in a radio broadcast over station KOCS, Ontario, Calif., on Columbus Day, 1957. "There is no hope for the man who feels he has gone about as far as he can go in perfecting himself. It was Columbus' dissatisfaction that led (on his third voyage) to the discovery of a new continent. Dissatisfaction with the old way, with the poverty, the inequality, the stagnation of an old, tired order. After the colonies had been built, the frontier must be pushed ever westward. It was an unwillingness to be satisfied with the old way that led from the alchemist's mortar and pestle to great modern steel mills, to the whole new technological world of rocketry, medicine, and nuclear physics. Yet more important than this is the progress man must make in the development of the powers of the human spirit. It is here," the priest on the radio said, "that there is indeed 'no hope for the satisfied man.' No hope for the man who doesn't want to be better." For the dissatisfied spiritual adventurer, for the explorer of the capes of human ability and the peninsulas of imagination and achievement, for the man who will not be satisfied until he has achieved a new existence (St. Paul's phrase), already begun now but to be climaxed in the beautiful New World with the Great Captain — for this man and all like him, God has given the Mass. The greatest human achievements are due to the Holy Sacrifice. It was a tiny caravel that took hawk-nosed Christopher Columbus to the promised land of teakwood and spices. It is the Mass which will bring the weary human traveler to that place where God Himself will complete all that was unfinished, all that was imperfect, all that was lacking in this great vibrant crucial experiment called "life."

In the cosmos of human affairs the priesthood of Christ stands out like the comet's fiery passage through the uncharted void. Its livid trail plots a route to God, its heat provides power for a resurrection from the gravity-pull of our tendencies to sin into a new galaxy where all things wheel in awesome order and dignity around the celestial focus of the universe, the Sacred Heart of Jesus. The love of that Heart warms the world. The Mass is perfect proof and expression of that love.

Psychiatry and the Mass

RELIGION stands like a towering ballistic missile, locked on its complex launching pad by a giant gantry tower of human emotions and aspirations. It points toward the heavens. Its aim is to launch a satellite (the human spirit) into a precisely determined orbit (union with God). The gantry tower bulking up like a giant oil derrick and the launching pad with its congeries of pipes, tanks and pumps, nozzles and valves, represent the complex of human motives, virtues, awareness of destiny, loves, sacrifices, and insights into the supernatural. When everything is working properly (and this is possible because of God's exquisite skill with this most involved of all satellite projects), religion will successfully launch the soul into its orbit.

But a small part out of kilter can upset the whole launching, perhaps a valve valued at but a few dollars.[1] Men skilled in the science of religion know that small things can prevent the soul from properly reaching its destiny, and sometimes altogether frustrate that aim. A most important element in the firing of this rocket is the mental stability of the individual human. Psychiatry, the science or art of healing mental ailments, works down in the spiderweb of machinery surrounding religion, setting right the complicated mechanism of the human mind and emotions. Healthy emotions and mentality do not guarantee a successful launching. Something else might go askew, like the equally crucial human will, for instance, which might choose evil instead of good. But religion without mental health is at best a cripple, at worst a great deceit and fizzle.

Chief fuel igniting the rocket of religion and driving it to its destination is the Mass. The Mass strengthens and acknowledges the link binding man with God. Religion provides that link; the Mass bolsters it. Because the Mass demands certain requirements of mind and will from the humans to whom God has entrusted it, it also has a tie with psychiatry. Psychiatry remotely assists men to offer the Mass well. The Mass gives humans the tools to build sound mental states, perhaps in conjunction with the psychiatrist.

God builds on our nature as it is; if the foundation of will is weak, if the pilings of determination are not driven deep enough, then there is danger of future unhappiness.

---

[1] Malfunctioning of a $35 valve caused the failure of one Atlas firing, a several million dollar project. One valve failed to operate properly at extremely low temperature caused by lox (liquid oxygen) fuel.

Meditating on the Passion (= sufferings of Christ) has a psychological effect and a therapeutic effect. Most humans — all of them fundamentally — want to be loved. They need to be loved! (God planted the desire for appreciation and love in each human heart, because He knew that later He would fill this desire!) The Mass is a grand meditation on the sufferings of Christ, and a re-enactment of them. The Mass is an expression of God's love for you.

Even a little bit of meditation on Christ's sufferings does you some great good, because it is the greatest kind of love that you will ever have. Down deep you know that, and everybody knows that, even though at times certain ones may pretend, and try to deceive themselves that they think some other human can love them more.

When you go to Mass you see this tremendous representation of God's love for you. You are able to regain your self-value, a proper view of your own worth. You say to yourself, "If God values me so much that He offers and sacrifices His life for me, I cannot be such a miserable heel as I sometimes think I am. There must be some good in me, at least the chance to develop some good qualities. I have gone off and acted like a fool (when I sinned), but God must see something in me that is worth while. I guess I'll try again to act better. I must not be altogether rotten, as some have told me I was."

When you compliment a person, he responds by brightening up a little. For example, if you tell grandma that she looks better today, she straightens up a bit and smiles, and she *feels* better too. The Mass is a compliment spoken by God. He says: "You are dear to Me; I offer My life for you. I think you are worth while. I think you are valuable. I know you are valuable. You look good to Me."

Dr. Etienne Grosjean, prominent Catholic psychiatrist in a

large eastern city, stated in an interview his belief in an extraordinarily close kinship between psychiatry and the Mass.

Dr. Grosjean, you served with the navy during the last war. Did you find that there were fewer Catholics among the mentally ill?

Yes. I remember that among the psychiatric patients in mental hospitals where I worked, there was a smaller percentage of Catholics, as compared with the over-all percentage of Catholics in the navy.

What do you think was the reason for this, doctor?

I credit it to the wonderful outlook most Catholics have. They had an easier time with guilt complexes, frustrations, suffering. Their faith equipped them with a built-in altruism, one of the best weapons against mental illness. They realized more vividly the providence of God, working out their lives and bringing beauty out of the tangled skein of seemingly unrelated, purposeless events. The Mass and sacraments gave them a do-it-yourself-kit for achieving peace of heart. All of their desires, it is true, were not fulfilled. But they knew that life is not wasted. Even their sufferings were gold for supernatural barter.

How much influence do you think the Mass had on their lives?

A great deal, primarily from the viewpoint of grace. I believe the Church has something definite on that point in Session 22 of the Council of Trent. But the Mass also has strong therapeutic value in terms of emotional control.

Do you think God designed the Mass and its ceremonial with man's emotional health in mind?

Of course, He had the whole man in mind, emotions as well as mind and will. The Mass liturgy powerfully affects the imagination and affective life. God does not set aside the natural means which can help the imagination and emotions. All these means are His own invention.

You would say that God uses the tools of the psychiatrist in building souls into living temples of the Holy Spirit?

Rather just the reverse. God knows and uses perfectly the means which some lucky psychiatrist stumbles upon by accident or reasons out piecemeal and applies falteringly. What we psychiatrists have figured out is, as St. Paul reminds us, only a distorted image of the reality. Still it is an image and for that reason important. God with supreme skill and perfect comprehension has been applying these means fully. Since the Mass is the summation of all that is good in the world of spirit and matter, we would be surprised if it left out some important items for improving mankind. We would be amazed if the Mass failed to incorporate all the means of curing the human spirit.

Would you care to elaborate a little, doctor?

It seems to me that we humans have an obligation to free ourselves from emotional instability. We are arriving at some astonishing conclusions regarding the origin of disease. Some investigators have asked if some sort of emotional or psychic stress triggers *all* disease. There is a good deal of evidence inclining them to this hypothesis. A careful, protracted study of tuberculosis patients reveals a startling link with emotional instability. The Ochsner Clinic in New Orleans, after close study of 500 victims of gastrointestinal diseases, discovered that 74 per cent of them were suffering from emotion-induced illnesses.

Then by curing our emotional problems, we can cure our bodily ills?

Well, some of them anyhow. Recent studies point in that direction. Emotional factors may play as important a role as a virus in causing common colds. The mother's anxieties often express themselves in her children in the form of asthma, colitis, even stomach aches.

What about emotions causing TB? That sounds fantastic.

Dr. Thomas H. Holmes of Seattle, a practicing psychiatrist, told the American College of Chest Physicians in Manhattan in 1957 that more than 50 per cent of 1500 TB victims in his study came from homes marred by divorce, death, or a separation of the parents before the victim was 18 years old. He characterized tuberculars as shifting from one job, from one place, and from one husband to another. The divorce rate among them is four times the U. S. average. From 20 to 25 per cent of them had psychoses, 36 per cent neuroses. Ill at ease in their environment, they struggled to adjust and the attempt produced, Dr. Holmes reported, "unrealistic striving, cumulative conflict, anxiety, and depression." It would seem that when the patient's limited abilities to solve his problems or get satisfaction were exhausted, TB appeared. And that isn't all. A Bristol, England, University psychologist, Denis H. Stott, in a study of 102 mentally retarded children, found that 67 came from pregnancies troubled by severe emotional strain. Now it might be that the mother's emotional upset caused the child's mental retardation. Even lowly acne appears to be caused in part by emotional factors.

How does the Mass cure mental sickness?

Let me give you an example. A high school senior came to me once, suffering from periodic pains in one knee. He had been in a minor automobile accident about a month before, and the pains had showed up two or three weeks later. He was sent to a neurologist by his family doctor. When neither of them could find any reason for the pains, they asked the boy to see me. I found him to be of above-average intelligence, attractive, athletic, and in the middle of a severe emotional and moral crisis. He was indecisive, a fairly hard worker but an aimless one. His life lacked purpose, emotional control was not notably present.

What did you advise this fellow?

In the course of a dozen interviews I assisted him to reason out goals for himself. I said that a three-year hitch in the service was only a minor obstacle, or even could be considered a great period of learning new skills. And I stressed the capabilities he had for achieving important goals. I encouraged him to see what was to be gained by understanding himself. Then I pointed out obstacles: sloth, carelessness, unwillingness to make the necessary sacrifices. I threw in abundant stories of men who overcame great obstacles, both in their environment and in their own personalities. And I frequently mentioned how daily Mass helps us form and achieve a goal, how it had helped me through the years. We struck up quite a friendship and I found out that he began attending daily Mass. There was a striking change in a few weeks. He was more at ease, made rapid progress in overcoming emotional immaturity, improved his school work, and became a much easier person to live with, his delighted parents told me.

Do you think daily Mass caused this change?

In large part, yes. Whether we psychiatrists like to think so or not, the greatest changes in human conduct, the lasting turns for the better, the really permanent turnings over of new leaves, are products of the grace of God, not of the skill of a psychiatrist. We are in some fashion instruments of that grace. Many psychoanalytical techniques can be means of assisting the flow of divine grace into the human soul, since they help make the faculties apt for co-operating with that supernatural life of grace. The syndrome Catatonic schizophrenia on the psychological level is a mental withdrawal from life's difficulties. In a wider plane it is an obstacle to an individual's growth in the Christ-life. I am as a psychiatrist concerned professionally with the syndrome. But I am not unaware of my secondary role as abettor of grace. I help grace work in a soul by assisting a patient to free himself of certain mental and emotional blocks; grace at the same time catalyzes my therapy. It plays the more important part. That is why I commonly recommend frequent attendance at Mass to Catholic patients.

Would you say the Mass inspired a man to obtain certain helps by which he can have peace of mind? Does the Mass, in other words, promote peace of mind as do other holy spectacles, watching the martyrs die, for instance?

No. The various blessings a man asks for at Mass and which the Council of Trent refers to as "other necessities" are obtained by the very offering of the Mass itself, independently of my own efforts. Of course we are presuming that I place no obstacle in the path of these effects — for instance, by remaining in the state of mortal sin.

Then the Mass obtains peace of mind ex opere operato, *on its own merits, although not infallibly?*

Yes, there are always two important questions: (1) is the thing we are asking for really best for our soul's salvation. Sometimes, perhaps more often than we realize, anxieties and frustrations help us get closer to Christ. (2) When I attend Mass and ask for peace of mind, I need certain dispositions so that the Mass can produce the effect in me.

Cardinal Billot, I believe, says that as regards these dispositions, a man must not only be free of habitual mortal sin but must want to be free of all sin. Conscious of his inadequacy, he views the sacrifices required of him in the light of faith, as small payment for the priceless gifts of God. Doctor, aren't

126

very good results achieved by psychoanalysis without any re-course to the Mass?

By all means yes. And the great work of many psychiatrists is proof of that. But how much better results could be achieved by these techniques plus the Mass! The Mass gives grace and grace aids our intelligence. Mature understanding of ourselves is essential for achieving mental health. And, as I have said, the Mass helps us gain emotional control. It does this via grace and via suggestion and other psychological avenues unknown to us. This emotional control in turn aids intelligence. Some today think that intelligence depends more on our emotional control and adaptability than on knowledge. Dr. Menninger observed an 11-year-old's I.Q. rise from 65 to 90[2] in a three-year period with psychiatric treatment. So the Mass, by helping us achieve emotional maturity, again is assisting intelligence.

Precisely how does the Mass, apart from actual grace, help us gain control of our emotions, doctor?

There is a reference somewhere in the *Spiritual Exercises* of St. Ignatius to the usefulness of praying with a rhythm, as of breathing, and of speaking some parts of a vocal prayer in rhythmic fashion, with each breath we take. Now in the calming process of breathing and following some easy rhythm, there is a frame of mind induced, or its formation assisted. This process is especially true of the Mass. For those who are aware of its value, most of all. But even for those who are not. There is a rhythm in the Mass, a rhythm in its rubrics guiding the movements of the priest on the altar, a grand, sublime rhythm in its calm, majestic prayers. In the Mass there is found consummate order. In the Mass we see actions directed to a great

---

[2] Perhaps he had the I.Q. of 90 to begin with, but was able to function only at a 65 level. Still, there is some significance here.

goal: the consecration. We see individual whim of the priest subjected to the transcendent rule of the liturgy. It doesn't matter if we are up or down, jubilant or miserable, worried or at peace. The Mass always proceeds at the same noble pace. Its prayers are never shrill and frantic. Its movements never raucous or frenzied. It has a profoundly calming effect. My day starts on an uneven keel if I can't get to morning Mass, so I have to scout around to find an evening Mass. The calming effects of the Mass tone the whole man, too, make him better in every way.

How is that, doctor?

Emotions are mental states that cause bodily changes. Severe anger is often followed by stomach pains. The mental state has caused the muscles of the stomach to contract and this contraction upsets digestion. Pulse and blood pressure rise sharply in a fit of temper, and may even cause a heart attack. Many pains such as muscular rheumatism and fibrositis can be traced to emotions, as can about thirty per cent of skin ailments (neurodermatitis), headaches, even cramps. The Mass, by helping us stabilize our emotional life, soothes and stabilizes the entire body with its intricate muscular system.

Doctor, it sounds very strange to hear a psychiatrist tie up the Mass and psychiatry so closely as you have done today. I had always thought somehow that religion and psychiatry were antagonistic.

There has been antagonism, with a good deal of suspicion arising in the camp of religion. And there was reason for it. Some psychiatrists, more especially in the field of psychoanalysis, disagree radically with Catholic teaching on such matters as the nature and destiny of man and moral law. Freud himself, the founder of psychoanalysis, was victim of three errors which are to be found among some of his followers to this day. He

was a materialist who disbelieved in the world of spirit. . . .
Second, Freud was an atheist. Obviously he had to junk belief
in God since God is spirit and Freud would have none of
spirit. . . . And Freud, finally, was a determinist. He denied
that man has a free will and sought explanation for man's
actions in other forces over which man has no control. . . .

*Does this mean that psychoanalysis is forbidden to Catholics,
doctor?*

No. Catholics may practice or submit to psychoanalytic treatment provided no immoral means are used. Despite Freud's
obscurantist hostility to religion and Christianity in particular,
his psychoanalytical methods have much value. Not everyone
agrees with this statement, by the way. Dr. Frederic Wertham
of New York maintains that six out of every ten psychoanaly-
ses do more damage than good. And a sizable contingent of
psychologists and psychiatrists challenges some of the basic
theories of depth psychology on scientific grounds.

*A Catholic, or any conscientious Christian, ought to be care-
ful in his choice of an analyst.*

Certainly, just as he is careful in his choice of a physician
or confessor. Because of the nature of the analyst's work, dealing with the unconscious and the nature of various emotional
drives, his mistakes will have terrible repercussions. Very great
caution is in place in selecting an analyst. I believe that far
fewer Catholics would find themselves in a position to pick one,
if they fully appreciated and used the Mass. At Mass our
attention is turned to the truths of God's providence. The Mass
is itself an illustration of the extreme means which God uses
to take care of us, not to leave us "orphans," but to be with
us intimately. "Having loved His own to the end," He would
love them even beyond the end, beyond His death. No! He
would cancel out death, so that He would be living with us

in the Mass. Our emotions are calmed by this terrific reassurance.

It is a radical new idea, doctor.

Oh no, not at all. There is, as you know, a view in the field of art criticism today that the purpose of art is physical, mental, and moral healthfulness. This isn't really surprising. Men of this persuasion, such as artist-critic Theodore Shaw, hold with Thomas Aquinas that beauty is "that which gives pleasure." Since man is a unit, that pleasure must necessarily influence the whole man. Aesthetic pleasure has a kinship with nerves, worries, longevity. Good art makes for better health and a longer life. It benefits the whole man, body and soul, not just some isolated, hypothetical fragment of him termed "aesthetic sense."

Would you tie this theory to the Mass?

I have been working something out along those lines, yes. As a psychiatrist I am professionally committed to my patients' mental health. But I cannot dispense with nor ignore their physical and moral health. All three are embodied in the same individual and are inextricably tied together. Every psychiatrist must first gain his M.D. degree for this very reason, that he can diagnose bodily ills in mentally disturbed patients if such be present. We have heard a lot about mental sickness causing bodily sickness. But that is a two-way street. Bodily sickness can and does cause mental imbalance. So in treating illness, a man must be prepared to diagnose on three separate levels: the bodily, as a medical doctor, the psychological as a psychiatrist, and the moral, as a kind of spiritual adviser, at least to the extent possible to a layman.

Do you think, Doctor Grosjean, that the Mass functions on these three levels?

Yes, I think it does. It certainly functions on the moral

level. The very formula the priest uses in consecrating the wine contains the words "for the remission of sin." The Mass not only makes reparation for sin in terms of humanity, but it infallibly gives the grace we need to be sorry for sin in terms of the individual sinner. The graces of the Mass are indispensable for avoiding sin and being positive and progressive in growing in the virtues. The Mass functions on the bodily level indirectly through its effect on emotions and the mental state of a man.

What about the Mass's psychological effects, doctor? Does it have any and how pronounced are they?

It is here that I think the Mass can be considered in terms of its aesthetic elements. It has poetry in the sequences of the Mass. It has music, some of the most beautiful in the world. Gregorian chant has a particularly calming influence. The Mass utilizes rhythmic movement, and I suppose by a stretch of the imagination we could refer to this as something from the dance. Recently an entire book of photographs was published, dealing merely with the priest's hands during the Mass. The Holy Ghost is responsible for the development of the liturgy, and I think that fact enhances its therapeutic value. God, who formed this complexly articulated human spirit, knows best by what routes it may be reached and influenced. We speak today of subliminal perception, a technique of advertisers, which makes use of audio or visual images which can be perceived but not consciously. When this technique was tried on 45,000 people in a New Jersey motion picture theater, popcorn sales jumped 59 per cent. There are a lot of subliminal perceptions in the Mass, various postures of pleading, asking forgiveness, humility. There are the priest's glances at the crucifix, his globular motion with the hands indicating the tremendous sweep of the Mass. These intuitions and insights are subliminal in this sense, that we receive them and their influence without consciously adverting to them at all times.

Then you don't think God was surprised by this new advertising technique, eh doctor?

If there was any surprise, it was rather that it took us so long to become cognizant of something He has long since put into His liturgy. The other rites contain similar techniques. In the Armenian liturgy priest and deacon after the consecration lie down flat on the ground. The celebrant in the Coptic rite prostrates twice before the sacred Elements, and the priest in the Chaldean liturgy bows low to the Blessed Sacrament. In each case we have an external expression of adoration, dependence, trust, hope. The culture of various peoples may demand some different type of expression, as we have seen here. But each gesture and movement expresses a profound interior sentiment, and — what is more to the point now — inculcates that sentiment in those witnessing it, though they are unaware of it. Children see their parents kneel to the tabernacle, receive Communion devoutly; they witness a vivid, intricate wheel of ceremonial pivoting on one Thing, Christ in the Eucharist. This teaches them a tremendous amount in areas we hardly even suspect. But the Church more than suspects. Hence the law to attend Mass on Sundays and holydays. The "born Catholic" is a very lucky individual. All through his formative, impressionable years he is exposed to these perceptions in the liturgy. Belief in Jesus' reality in the Eucharist is rooted in the very depths of his psychological machinery.

Then you would say, Doctor Grosjean, that the liturgy is not superimposed from without but grows from within our culture.

Isn't that truth borne out by a comparative study of the

various liturgies? The Eastern rites generally have a more stately, more majestically paced Mass. While the tempo of our Roman Mass, on the contrary, which is common in the most advanced and technological of our nations, is staccato. Our society is staccato, so the liturgy is staccato. Oriental peoples, in their worship at least are demonstrative, more ceremonious than we. Their liturgy rises from these traits in them. Our Latin Rite appeals peculiarly to us, with its straight-forward, Roman-law simplicity and directness. The ceremonial jewel in which the essence of the Mass is set has evolved out of the needs and characteristics of various peoples, and in turn the liturgy that develops continues these traits and expresses these needs into the next generations. The Mass is truly a tie uniting one age with the next.

Doctor, what made you give so much thought to this close tie between the Mass and psychiatry?

My own experience, I think. Especially when I was studying medicine. I suffered greatly from pains in the neck and in the back of the head. They proved to be emotional in origin, tension, nervousness. A wise old priest directed me to the Mass, and to a calm, relaxed participation in it. He told me that some mental difficulties are cured when their origin is discovered to the sufferer, and he applied this to the Mass. He said that the Mass helps us know ourselves, our hidden motives, the worthwhileness of duty, the nobility of work, the advantage to suffering, the true goal of life, the profit in self-sacrifice. The tension left me and hasn't been back since, and with it went the pains and the sleepless nights. I have since learned that 85 per cent of such pains are emotional in origin, and you are aware, of course, of the damage done to the stomach and other organs by anxiety as expressed in the peptic ulcer.

Can the Mass then cure bodily ailments, doctor?

Yes, indirectly. If such ailments are mental or emotional in origin, they can usually be cured by touching their source. I have helped relieve patients suffering from spastic colon, irritable colon, nonspecific ulcerative colitis, abdominal pain, migraine headaches, skin ailments, dizziness, and fainting spells by exposing the emotional conflicts in which these ills had taken root, and helping the patient resolve them. When the emotional stress was relieved, the illness disappeared.

Perhaps this may explain why the saints were so long-lived.

There isn't any doubt that emotional balance, something the saints all possessed, goes far toward giving us good health and a long life. I have noted that the saints eliminated three of the four causes of arteriosclerosis as stated by Osler, namely, sexual pleasure, drinking, and the use of tobacco. To a great extent we are as old as our arteries.

Then the good don't all die young.

Quite the opposite. Of some 280 saints formally canonized by the Holy See, two lived past 100, four were in their 90's, 15 in their 80's, 44 in their 70's, 58 in their 60's, and 36 in their 50's. Two thirds lived past 50. And these men and women lived long before antibiotics, skillful surgical techniques involving such things as kidney transplant and heart surgery. The saints, I think, discovered the secret of optimal hormone balance, and they all had a tremendous love of the Mass. I am firmly convinced of a causal connection here. The Mass satisfies all that is noblest and most beautiful in the human heart.

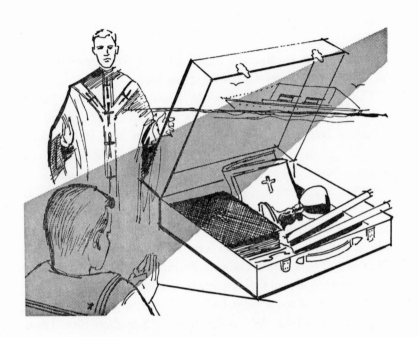

His "Do-It-Yourself" Cathedral

"Now hear this," bellowed the loud-speakers aboard the cruiser *U.S.S. Houston.* "Rig for Mass on the quarter deck. Confessions will be heard in the port hangar at oh-six-hundred. All you sick, lame, and wicked lay up there on the double."

Piped aboard by a chief boatswain's mate on watch, Christ visited a vessel of the United States Navy, the cruiser *Houston.* A choir of angels had done the trick for the shepherds, telling of the coming of Christ, and a star tipped off the wisemen. Now a chief boatswain was doing the job of star and Seraphim. The *Houston* went down under a hail of shells in the Java Sea in World War II. But the sacrifice of the Mass goes on and on, penetrating every level of human life.

The reason for this is that the Mass is, simply, the "most holy and divine" of all the works that can be performed by a human being (Council of Trent, Session 22). It has to be valuable, because it is Christ's. Otherwise, why should priests brave so many dangers to bring the Mass to their flocks?

Father (Lieutenant Commander) Edward R. Martineau is an example. He is "the most traveling chaplain in the Navy," according to Chaplain (Capt.) Jim Kelley, Southern Baptist. The genial Benedictine made forty highline transfers in recent Operation Tradewinds. On this Pacific jaunt he also engaged in his own miniature Operation Six Sunday Masses.

"We were en route from Japan to the States," he said, "due to stop at Honolulu. 'We' is Amphibious Squadron Five. I was chaplain of that outfit at the time (Easter, 1957). When we crossed the International Date Line we picked up an extra day. Because we crossed on Sunday, Easter Sunday, we picked up an extra Sunday. According to the needs of their men, all military chaplains can offer three Masses on Sunday and two on one other day of the week, at their own choice. I planned to say two Masses on Holy Saturday, and three each on 'both' Easter Sundays. That would make a total of eight Masses, one on each of the eight ships of our squadron. The ships were the *Calvert*, the *Magoffin*, the *Montrose*, the *Telfair*, now in the mothball fleet, the *Weiss*, the *Diachenko*, the *Skagit*, and the *Algol*."

Father Martineau began his "Operation Six Sunday Masses" on schedule, transferring from ship to ship in a breeches buoy, a tricky, sometimes dangerous procedure. On a line strung from one ship across the open sea to a second ship running close along side, Father Martineau, snuggled in a small chair, was hauled across the deep swells from ship to ship of Amphibious Squadron Five. On Holy Saturday he offered two Masses and on the "first" Easter Sunday the scheduled three. But after the intrepid chaplain had offered one Mass on the "second" Easter Sunday, heavy seas called a halt to "Operation Six Sunday Masses."

Father Martineau, now stationed in Rhode Island with a Naval Construction Battalion (Seabees), remarks: "I'm still at it. Up one gangplank and down another, lugging three or four bags, a tape recorder, and Mass kit (my do-it-yourself Cathedral)."

Reason for the priest's eagerness to bring the Mass to his people lies in what the Mass can do. Toward the end of the Middle Ages (thirteenth and fourteenth centuries), writers trying to catalog the effects of the Mass compiled lists of "fruits" sometimes mounting into the hundreds.[1] It is not possible to attend the representation of the Sacrifice of Calvary without great spiritual profit.

Commented a pastor whose parish had been rejuvenated by heavy attendance at daily Mass: "Focusing on the profit the Mass brings may be called spiritual utilitarianism. But if the Mass were not useful to us, why go? And we do have Scriptural precedent for thinking about reward. St. Paul wrote to Philippi, 'Intent on what lies before me, I press on with the goal in view, eager for the prize' (3:13, 14). A lot of my people had thought of attending Mass as simply a manifestation of their faith. Something like a pilgrimage. Now that they have found out that the Mass does more good for them than anything else the Church has to offer, they are flocking to Mass."

---

[1] Josef A. Jungmann, *The Mass of the Roman Rite* (New York: Benziger Bros., 1950), Vol. 1, p. 129.

Typical of the long lists of effects of the Mass is one in what is probably the most famous book ever written on the Holy Sacrifice. In *An Explanation of the Mass,* a venerable Capuchin monk named Martin von Cochem ticked off seventy-seven fruits, or ways by which the soul benefits from hearing Mass. Samples: Grace is increased, venial sins forgiven, material blessings gained, our purgatory shortened, God perfectly honored, souls in purgatory helped. Yet while such lists multiplied, they did not begin to exhaust the effects of the Mass. We have in recent times begun to suspect that the powers of our nature are far greater than previously thought. Whether strange phenomena like luminosities, levitations, and telekinesis, are attributed to poltergeists or the *psi*-factor, it remains true that human nature has depths not yet sounded. Of course the Mass utilizes all these potentialities of human nature. It arouses us to sorrow for sins, forgives venial sins, removes the temporal punishment we have coming for our past sins, soothes and calms, and even gives a sense of fellowship, so prized by non-Catholics.

The news editor of a Mountain States daily paper, who became a Catholic in middle age, remarked that attending Mass helped him escape the sense of loneliness and enkindled a spirit of comradeship with other worshipers and with the whole Church. "No matter where I go to Mass," he remarked, "I know that *all* of us in the congregation are doing great things together, from the little lady in the front pew to me in the back one. We are all *actively* working for one another's good. At Mass I am actively sharing in the offering of Jesus to His Father. I sit there quietly and know that I am doing more for myself, for my family, for the Church, than by any other activity."

Extraordinary is the Mass's influence. As he offers up the

host, the priest breathes a silent prayer which beautifully expresses this influence. Like a multiple-stage rocket the prayer rises dizzyingly to greater and greater heights, driven by the burning love of Christ. First stage: the Mass helps the priest. Second stage: it helps all who attend (*circumstantibus*). Third stage: it helps all Christians. Fourth stage: even the dead profit from the Mass. And what does the Mass do for these galaxies of souls? Affords them hope of eternal life. Union with God is the goal of the Mass, the satellite put into everlasting orbit around the divine Trinity.

What else spurs on the white-clad Divine Word missionary through the jungles of India to a remote village of Jhirpani? What else makes him so eager to renew the sacrifice of Calvary at a makeshift altar hemmed in by banana groves and rock-studded hills? For love of these Munda, Oraon, and Khariya tribesmen, the missionaries brave steaming, rain-soaked tangles of vine and brush. Only the Mass could bring them to do it, for it alone offers hope to man of escaping the labyrinthine jungles of his own fears and passions.

The Roman proconsul trying the Abitina martyrs for their lives on charges of being Christians, quizzed the prisoners about their attendance at Mass. The narrator of the Acts cannot help but exclaim: "As if a Christian could get along without the Mass."[2] Not only the individual Christian but the world cannot get along without the Mass.

Realization of the power of the Mass to forgive sins led in the tenth and eleventh centuries to the insertion into the Mass prayers of frequent and endless avowals of personal guilt and unworthiness called *apologiae*. In time the apologiae were dropped for the most part. The Mass gains us forgiveness of venial sin and contrition for mortal sin independently of such

---

[2] *Ibid.* ("Quasi Christianus sine dominico esse possit."), p. 173, footnote 33.

avowals.[3] Sin is the negative element keeping us from union with Jesus Christ. The Mass removes the negative element, and stimulates the positive, increasing in us grace and the virtue of charity by which we and God are united.

How practical the Mass is! The noted German liturgist, Father Kramp, once observed that "the liturgy is not intended as a beautiful play of symbols; its purpose is to effect a real union of the soul with Christ."[4] "How unfortunate it would be," said a Norbertine educator, "if we should become entangled in verbalities about the Mass and fail to practice in our lives the principles the Mass inculcates." Outstanding is the Eucharist-centered life of the Norbertines. They stress both the Eucharist as sacrifice (= Mass) and the Eucharist as sacrament (= Communion), an endowment inherited from their great founder St. Norbert.

Said a famous canon lawyer, "All the virtues are increased in us and we gain a prodigious share of grace through the power of the Mass." Pope Innocent III (1198–1216), styled "greatest medieval pope," lived this teaching. He had one ecclesiastical eye trained on France's dallying, twice-married King Philip II and on England's luckless King John. (When rebellious nobles forced the Magna Charta on John, Innocent promptly annulled it as having been extorted by force.) With the other eye the pope kept tab of his own libertinous, but gifted protégé Frederick II (excommunicated in 1227 by Pope

---

[3] One of the causes, according to Father Jungmann, *op. cit.* (Vol. I, p. 80), for the proliferation of the *apologiae* in the Mass of the Roman Rite was a lack of appreciation of the value of frequent confession. As late as the eleventh century most monks as well as laymen went to confession only once a year. Today we know that frequent confession is one of the chief means of establishing close union with God. Hence the disappearance of the *apologiae*. But this knowledge does not lessen the Mass's power to wipe away sin.

[4] Joseph Kramp, S.J., *Live the Mass* (St. Paul: Catechetical Guild Society, 1954), p. 123.

Honorius III) and of Otto of Brunswick, whom he himself excommunicated in 1210. Yet in such feverish affairs of state, Innocent was mindful of the power of the Mass. It gave him strength to carry on his work in union with God.

The Catholic must be, to use a phrase of Father Jerome Nadal's, at the same time contemplative and active (*simul in actione contemplativus*). Father Nadal, one of the first disciples of St. Ignatius Loyola, explained the saint's views on prayer this way: strenuous activity for and in Christ must be, not a distraction from but a means to closer union with God.[5] The Mass especially finds the right formula for blending work and reflection on God. "Make our wills," pleads the Secret for the Mass of the Fourth Saturday of Lent, "even though they are rebellious, turn toward You (Christ)." The Mass directs the energies of our will toward God by revealing to us that perfect Goodness and Lovableness of Christ. The richness and beauty of the Divine Person of Christ are the focal point of the Mass.

"People in general," a consulting psychologist remarked, "use only about 12 to 15 per cent of their brain's capabilities. Their happiness often lies in the development of the remaining 85 per cent. Failure and unhappiness are not infrequently the result of lazy minds." The Mass need never replace the laboratory of the experimental psychologist, but it can and does develop brilliantly the raw resources of the human spirit.

An educator in a Missouri Medical Center, who has had considerable success in developing the abilities of retarded students, compares the human mind to the earth's potentialities for producing goods. "Look at Africa. With one-fifth of the

---

[5] Joseph F. Conwell, S.J., *Contemplation in Action* (Spokane, Wash.: Gonzaga University, 1957). Doctoral dissertation subtitled: "A Study in Ignatian Prayer."

world's land surface, Africa manages to provide only three per cent of the world's exports of raw materials. Yet it could grow about every crop conceivable. It has the world's largest potential reservoir of water power. But only one per cent of it has been produced. The student who comes to me is something like this. Each has great potentialities in one endeavor or another. My job is to unlock these powers. Better, to spark the student into tapping them by his own study and effort. Encouragement, showing him how to study, these do wonders. If we can kindle the glow of interest, our main task is done."

The Mass of St. Stanislas Kostka (who died at age 17) says aphoristically: "Being made perfect in a short time, he (Stanislas) fulfilled a long time." (*Consummatus in brevi, explevit tempora multa.*) Stanislas loved the Mass. Helped by it, he squeezed into 17 short years a superior brand of heroic holiness such as long lifetimes seldom account for. What is holiness? The hunter of holiness has got to know about his prey if he is to bring it down. Down in Johnson County, North Carolina, quail hunters stalk through recently harvested corn fields, and nose through the countless long leaf pine thickets, where coveys bullet into the blue in a bluster of wings. The hunters know where to look for their quarry. Where is the habitat of holiness? What are its feeding habits?

Theologians usually divide holiness into (1) moral and (2) physical. Holiness itself generally means union with God. Physical holiness refers to the amount of sanctifying grace one possesses. It is the more important of the two. Why? The grace we receive in life directly determines our happiness in heaven. Each new degree of grace, no matter how trifling it appears, is, in effect, a new eternity added on to our destiny. Hence the need for properly assessing each tiny degree of grace, for making much of each as a link in a chain of graces leading

142

to our salvation. Famed Francis Suarez[6] says the gift of final perseverance is "made up of many effective helps which are not given in a lump-sum but are handed out on successive, opportune occasions." Each such occasion is a stitch in the fabric of our destiny. One slipped stitch can throw the whole tapestry out of perspective.

Moral holiness may be described as the intensity or fervor with which one carries out his religious duties. It is a man's spiritual temperature, and has an important if indirect bearing on his acquiring sanctifying grace. It is clear that one who lacks moral earnestness will neglect the means of gaining grace (= physical holiness), even though he may not commit mortal sin. An aged priest might have an immense degree of physical holiness (from his frequent ministration of the sacraments and offering Mass), yet be remiss in his work, peevish, spiteful, lazy, jealous, and proud. His lack of moral holiness deprived him of vast fortunes in sanctifying grace lost. Sad words for him: It might have been. On the other hand, saints like Stanislas Kostka or Dominic Savio (died at age 15 in 1857), thanks to intensely high spiritual fervor (better, fever), in a brief span of years won holiness so eminent as to be canonizable. The Mass more than anything else exploits these rich veins of spiritual gold and supernatural uranium. It makes the goal clear, brings the Divine Model Christ into clear focus, stimulates, encourages, prods, cheers, admonishes, and even furnishes the divine fuel (grace) to keep the process active.

This quarrying of spiritual riches is not limited to the individual Christian. For the Mass also benefits the entire Mystical Body, Christ's Church. Just as the rainbow has many colors, so the Mass displays the myriad virtues of Christ for

---

[6] Francis Suarez, *De Gratia* (liber x, caput, 7, 4–18), publisher unknown; this book was taken out of a seminary library and is very old.

the benefit of the whole Church. The rainbow not only reaches up to the heavens but it bends down its avenue of color to touch the earth. *There* lies a pot of gold. The Mass, like the rainbow, reaches up to heaven and gathers Christ's many virtues, and then bends down and brings them to men. Here, at Mass, there does in reality lie a pot of gold, the graces of God. The Mass brings the violet of sorrow for sin, the red of charity, the white of purity, the green of hope, the vermilion of courage, the indigo of patience, the gold of faith, the amber of justice.

In *Mystici Corporis* Pius XII said that the Savior "began the building of the mystical temple of the Church when by His preaching He announced His precepts; He completed it when He hung glorified on the cross" (no. 27 of translation). The Mass is the unbloody sacrifice of Calvary. Does it not, then, somehow continue this completing of Christ's Mystical Body?

By a kind of supernatural instinct Catholics often recognize the value of the Mass. The 75-year-old Knights of Columbus, with more than one million members and an insurance program in force of around $700 million, make much of the K. of C. Communion Sunday. In the words of a K. of C. grand knight in Los Angeles, "We are a tremendous force for good with our fraternal, financial, and charitable programs. But it is by our profession of faith and personal example as Catholic gentlemen, especially in attending Mass, that we best participate in council activities."

St. Lawrence Justinian, the cheerful, farseeing first Patriarch of Venice, once advised: "Take a pair of scales and place in one all kinds of good works: prayers, fasts, vigils, mortifications, pilgrimages, what have you. In the other put a single Mass. Hold up the scales and you will see that the Mass altogether outweighs the other works. Why? Because in the Mass Christ is offered in whom dwells the fullness of the Godhead in His body and blood (as St. Paul says), and who possesses in His person an incomparable treasure of merits. His intercession alone is omnipotent."

Is it any wonder that Pius XII called the devout hearing of Mass the "chief duty and supreme dignity"[7] of Christians.

Bespectacled Father Ed Martineau, suspended in the bouncing breeches buoy, knew that the Mass meant most to the men of Amphibious Squadron Five. For the Mass is Christ operating in human hearts, getting the best out of people, helping them realize their fullest potential in the short space of a lifetime. It is not such a long way from Martin von Cochem's list of seventy-seven fruits of the Mass to the *Houston* bosun's sharp command, "Rig for Mass!" Both spring from kindling insight that the Mass gives most because it contains the limitless riches of Christ.

---

[7] *Mediator Dei*, No. 80 of Vatican Library translation.

More Than a Cup of Tea

THE priest *ascends* the altar to say Mass. Why not? Heights and summits have always been associated by man with God. The Greeks (some of them anyhow) thought their gods lived on Mount Olympus. Pagans commonly built their temples on the crests of hills. In the Old Testament, the phrase "high places" means altars of pagan sacrifice, places where pagans worshiped. Moses received the Ten Commandments atop Mount Sinai, and the writer of Exodus, chapter 15 (verse 17), observes that his people have been given "a home on the mountain God claimed as His own."

We can see farther from summits and peaks. They lift us above the tumult of the world toward serenity and silence.

It is easier to reflect on a mountaintop. When Alfred Wills, English jurist, planted his alpenstock in the snows on the lofty Wetterhorn in 1854, he carefully noted his impressions. "We felt," he recalled later, "as in the more immediate presence of him who had reared this tremendous pinnacle, and beneath the 'majestical roof' of whose deep blue heaven we stood."

Now, of course, God is everywhere, and not less in the stippled shadows of the valley than in the rarefied brilliance of the craggy summit. But perhaps He sometimes *seems* nearer up above. "If only the others could know," exulted Maurice Herzog on the summit of 26,493-foot Annapurna in the Himalayas. "Our mission was accomplished," he recorded. "But at the same time we had accomplished something infinitely greater. How wondeful life would become. What an inconceivable experience it is to attain one's ideal and, at the very same moment, to fulfill oneself. I was stirred to the depths of my being. Never had I felt like this — so intense and yet so pure."[1]

In the Mass, greatest summit on earth because closest to God, God *is* nearer, as near as He can be short of heaven. At the altar, lifted up above the floor of the church for all to see, a ceremony takes place. And more than a ceremony. Certainly it is man's greatest fulfillment of himself, a real accomplishment, which endows the soul with supernatural purity and is literally an inconceivable experience because produced from the infinite riches of the divine mind.

The Mass is more than a ceremony. It is *the* ceremony, rather a ceremonial sacrifice which ennobles mankind, and even the material world. There are all kinds of ceremonies. In Japan, the children put on their brilliant kimonos and high wooden clogs, with tiny bells inside, to celebrate their doll

[1] *Annapurna* by Maurice Herzog (New York: E. P. Dutton & Co., 1953), pp. 208, 209.

festival. And at the O-Bon festival in July, Buddhist Bonzes go in procession to bays and lakes to float little paper lanterns across the ripples, symbols of the souls of ancestors who are thought to visit them at this time; in the evening the Bonzes give a farewell ceremony to the rattle of drums and chant of Sutras, for the souls returning to the other world.

There is one ceremony of the Japanese which is quite colorful: the historic Tea Ceremony, an ancient practice imported from China and retaining still the Confucian stoicism by which one does not show his emotions and is never garrulous. Described by Robert Stemper, S.J., American studying at Eiko Gakuen, in Japan, the tea ceremony is "real art, a most exquisite art. The actual training and content of the ceremony are matters of no consequence in themselves; the supremely important matter is that the act be performed in the most perfect, most polite, most graceful, most charming *manner* possible."

The tea ceremony opens without gaudery. The guests arrive silently and shoelessly, wearing white *Tabi* (socks), and are ushered into the twelve-by-fourteen-foot tea chamber where each in turn will admire the painting the host has hung in the alcove (*Tokonoma*) especially for this occasion. Beneath it is a bouquet of flowers delicately arranged. These are the only decorations, nothing distracts. "This is the way of the Orient," says Mr. Stemper, "simplicity with keen sensibility for beauty."

The guest of honor takes his place nearest the Tokonoma, seated like the others on a straw mat, feet tucked under him in the approved fashion, the large toes crossing one another. The host brings in the tea bowls, tea, water ladle. Before entering he kneels, bows to the guests, then with mincing steps carries the paraphernalia to a small charcoal brazier on which an iron kettle of water boils merrily.

148

With infinite grace and economy of motion the host removes the lid from the kettle and places it on edge beside the brazier. He ladles hot water into a tea bowl, rinses it, pours the used water into a side receptacle, with a bamboo spatula dips some powdered green tea from the tea caddy, a highly laquered wooden box, into the bowl, adds water with the ladle, and then whips the tea into a froth with a little bamboo brush. Finally he lifts the tea bowl up with both hands and, turning it around twice (to put the prettiest edge in the direction of the guest), places it on the mat of the guest. All the while, Jesuit Stemper explains, a not-too-lively conversation is taking place, centering on the implements of the tea ceremony. "The history of tea bowls and other equipment is of great interest to experts and devotees of the tea ceremony."

Stemper sums it all up: "The whole of the art, as to detail, signifies no more than the making and serving of a cup of tea."

Not so the Mass. In the Mass matter is important. It is true that manner, how-it-is-done, is considered. There are rubrics which guide the priest and tell him where to place his hands, when to look at the crucifix, when to move to one side or the other of the altar. Nothing is left to chance. *Yet in the Mass it is the content that counts.*" For the Mass contains, and is, the unbloody sacrifice of the cross. The Mass is no mere "discipline in deportment"; it contains and is the mystic death of Christ. It is ceremonial, after the rich Oriental tradition. (Was not its founder a Jew of Asia Minor?) But into it "Christ poured forth the riches of His divine love for men."[2]

The Mass looks back.[3] (Trent calls it a "memorial" to Christ's

---

[2] Deferrari, *op. cit.*, p. 266. Council of Trent, Session xiii, chap. 2 (Denz. 875).   [3] *Ibid.*, p. 288. Sess. xxii, chap. 1 (Denz. 938).

149

death.) It looks to the present, and yields in the Sacrament of the Eucharist the food of man's daily life "as an antidote, whereby we may be freed from daily faults and be preserved from mortal sins." And it looks to the future, for it is "a pledge of our future glory and of everlasting happiness."[4] In the Mass God says, "Here I have given you a guarantee that you will enjoy Me forever, for I have given you the body and blood of My Son. Not only is this a pledge of that future payment, it is the first installment of it, a beginning already made in time of that happiness and union with Me that will be your joy in heaven."

There is ceremonial to the Mass, beautiful disciplined pageantry. How even that helps us! There is a hidden though profound effect on the mind of man produced by the pageantry and beauty that he sees before him in the Mass. The movies produce similar effects in a man. "They stir up in his own inner consciousness other notions which are more vivid and more moving (than the visions and imaginations elicited by the picture before him). That is why it often happens that the man in the audience sees things happen in the persons and events portrayed on the screen that may never have really occurred, but which he nevertheless recognizes as thoughts, desires, and fears that at one time or another he has profoundly felt deep within him. It is correct to say that the extraordinary power of films finds its deepest explanation in the basic structure of our psychical activities, and that a show is all the more powerful the more it stirs up these processes."[5]

The Mass is like that. What visions and imaginations it

---

[4] *Ibid.*, p. 267. Trent, sess. xiii, chap. 2 (Denz. 875).

[5] "The Movies and the Nature of Man," address of the late Pope Pius XII to representatives of the Italian film industry (*Ci torna sommamente* is the Italian name of this talk) given June 21, 1955, at an audience in the Vatican Basilica.

conjures up! Of Christ at the Last Supper, breaking and blessing bread and wine, giving them to His chosen eleven with words of infinite gravity, "This is my body, this is the chalice of my blood." Of Jesus dying on the cross and then embodying this redemptive death in the bloodless, mystic sacrifice of the Mass, which will "accomplish an eternal redemption" (Trent, Sess. xxii, 938). Of our duties to God and man. Of heaven, of order and plan, of the lovableness of God and virtue and grace, passing like an unseen current through the words and will of the priest and coming to rest in Christ's body and blood. The Eucharist, like a battery, immobilizes and contains the power and energy of Jesus, passing them on with tremendous force when we make contact with them in Holy Communion which contains "the power of unity and love" (Denz. 414).

Richard Weaver, brilliant educator from the University of Chicago and gifted writer, believes that our modern world suffers in particular from two evils which he calls fragmentism and presentism. By fragmentism, in Professor Weaver's estimate, we become specialists obsessed with some minute particle of reality, like the man Nietzsche cited who spent his life analyzing the brain structure of a leech. We confuse our specialty, necessarily restricted, with the world. By presentism we become so imbued with the "now" that we forget past and future. We fail to learn the lessons taught by the past and betray a lack of responsibility for what our deeds may cause in the future.

The Mass is the answer to both evils. It gives us the grace to see the whole picture, to put reality into an ordered mosaic, rounding out the edges. A businessman in St. Louis, Missouri, used to attend Mass in St. Francis Xavier's Church at St. Louis University. Though not a Catholic at the time, he continued attending daily Mass. "I found," he later told his

151

confessor, "that the Mass helped me to see the whole picture, to fit things together. I was able to put myself into the plan of God, and at last I knew where I was going. I became a Catholic, and I know I owe that grace to those Masses I heard daily in the College Church."

The Mass not only contains, and is, Christ's mystic death on the cross; it also prolongs His physical presence (under the form of bread and wine) and, in addition, prolongs the priesthood. It is the Mass that, as it were, activates the priesthood of Christ. For without a sacrifice, there are no priests acting as such, though Christ's priesthood is itself eternal. The Mass is the sacrifice of Calvary, applying the saving power of the cross "for the remission of those sins which we daily commit."[6] Hence the Mass binds into itself the past (Calvary), making it present and with it Christ's priesthood actively working; in the Eucharist it gives us an assurance of our heavenly future, an assurance which is also a down payment on the joys of the beatific vision.

What the world needs more than ever before is a courageous, unrelenting love of the Mass — love of the Mass and what it can do for us, what it has already done for the saints of God — love of the Mass as the reservoir of divine energy "that has overflowed upon us in a full stream of wisdom and discernment, to make known to us the hidden purpose of (God's) will" (Ephes. 1:8, 9). What the world needs more than ever before is heroic, man-sized love of Jesus in the Blessed Sacrament, that blazing, blast-furnace kind of love that engulfed the hearts of saints and left them pure, tempered, forging from poor iron a witness for Jesus quick and strong as an épée in the Master's grasp.

Tiny Lucia Abobora, the only living seer of the miracle of

---

[6] Deferrari, *op. cit.* Trent, sess. xxii, chap. 1.

Fatima, wept as only a child can, crouching in a great dark pew. "What is the matter, child?" asked Father Cruz kindly. "I can't make my First Communion," she sobbed. Father Cruz gently asked her about the catechism and was satisfied with her answers. He took her to the pastor, Father Pena, who was in the sacristy. "This child knows her doctrine better than many of the others who are going to receive," he said calmly. "But she is only six years old!" the pastor expostulated. Tactful, persistent, Father Cruz won his point, noting that the Church requires that a child, to make her First Communion, must have reached the *use* of reason, not the *age* of reason (7 years).

That is the kind of love of the Mass and Communion that the world needs; a love like that child's; a love to match, as much as possible, the love that Christ has for us. "He still loved those who were his own, whom he was leaving in the world, and he would give them the uttermost proof of his love" (Jn. 13:1) — to the uttermost end, yes, and even beyond, down through all the years, loving and serving our needs in the Mass and Blessed Sacrament. His love is all that we expect a true and perfect love to be. It draws us close to Him; makes us beneficiaries of his own life and happiness; reminds us of Him always, by the visible sign of His presence, the Eucharist; changes our contact with God into an exchange of affection and service. Exchange: "that love (of God) resides not in our showing any love for God, but in his showing love for us first, when he sent out his Son to be an atonement for our sins" (1 Jn. 4:10).

First God loved us, and gave us Christ. God's love, embodied in the Person of His Son, Jesus, and our love meet and mingle at Mass. At Mass there is the perfect and complete association of humans with almighty God. Yet the world does not love the Mass enough. Everything on earth owes its life to the sun. Every soul living the God-life of grace owes that life to the "sun of devotions," the holy Mass. The Mass entirely radiates grace, and it could make everybody saints if its "grace-energy" were used. The sun's energy that is poured on an ordinary umbrella in one hour would be enough to light up the entire city of New York for a whole year, if that energy could be totally converted into electricity. The sun sends out billions of units of energy each day: the Mass sends out billions of units of grace, enough to give strength to everyone to overcome all temptation, achieve every virtue, carry every cross as Christ wishes.

Today scientists are trying to devise a system for converting the sun's energy (in the form of heat) into electrical energy. Machines made of disks catch the heat from the sun, capture it, and store a fraction of it in batteries. This electrical current then lights lights and runs machines. Now, the grace energy of the Mass can be captured too and converted into energy to light up our lives with acts of all the virtues, to operate our minds and wills after the manner of Christ Jesus. Our attending Mass devoutly is the way we have of capturing the grace energy, just as the machines made of disks do. The conversion of grace into a dynamically operating entity in our lives is accomplished by our free will, working in and with Christ.

Holy Mass is vacation for the human spirit. Generator of grace, it provides endless refreshment and solace for harassed and niggling humans. From the Mass, mountaintop of divine wisdom, we can survey peacefully the puzzling topography of our destiny, and make out design and order and God's infinite charity and mercy there. The swelling hummocks of hope and the canyons and ravines of suffering and separation blend into a landscape formed by God's loving hand, when they are viewed from the vantage point of the Mass. Petty irritations are no

longer visible in that gigantic panorama. Only the major land-
marks bulk out above the horizon: God's consuming love and
Christ's example, our duty, the nobility of work, the power
of kindness, the success of perseverance, the dignity of character, the need for the Mass.

The Mass is no tea party. But it is a meal, a sacrificial meal,
prepared by Chef Christ for hungry human hearts. How important is Mass? So important that "the work of the Catholic
Church in the world might be briefly described as getting
people to come to Mass."[7] How right the distinguished editor
of *Worship,* the Rev. Godfrey Diekmann, O.S.B., is when
he says that he and his colleagues "have consistently inter-
preted (liturgical worship) to mean: the theology of the sacraments (the Eucharist above all!) applied in practice to the
spiritual life. We have stressed the essentials: praying and living
with the Church, for the greater honor of God."[8] The Mass,
after all, is the heart of the liturgy; hence, the heart of human
life. For human life should be an extension into our daily
lives of the graces and lessons learned at Mass. The Mass
teaches, inspires, and strengthens; it enables us to "live our
faith."

"Say a Mass for us, Father," whispered a spectacled workman with tired eyes, pressing a crumpled dollar bill into the
priest's hand. "The doctor just told me and my wife that he
got the report on the X rays he took of my wife's lungs, and
she is full of cancer. She has less than six weeks to live. The
blood tests showed that the cancer is in her blood." Say a Mass
for us, Father! Here lies exposed the Catholic's instinctive
turning to the Mass for help and consolation. How often a

---

[7] Canon F. H. Drinkwater, *Educational Essays* (London: Burns, Oates,
1951), p. 134.

[8] *Worship* (April, 1957), Vol. 5, lines quoted from the back of front
cover, written by Rev. Godfrey Diekmann, O.S.B., editor of *Worship.*

tragic case of some suffering loved one prompts the words full of faith, "Say a Mass for us, Father."

And the Mass, if it does not bring a miracle, will bring the needed grace to see that God in great wisdom (now not seen but to be apparent later on) has sent this suffering, just as He sent the suffering to Mary at the cross.

Say a Mass for us, Father — for us, the millions who labor in the vineyards and factories, in the mills and plants, in the shops and offices, in the kitchens and terminals of a taut, tempestuous life. Sometimes, it is the anxious care for the spiritual welfare of our sons or daughters that sends us to you with "Say a Mass for us" on our lips. Whatever it is, we turn first, last, and always to the Mass, as our surest source of help. We may not be able to express all this in a very fancy way. But we know what it means, perhaps darkly and obscurely but surely, when we come to you and say, "Say a Mass for us, Father."

The Mass Catholics are familiar with today is essentially nothing more than the sacrificial changing of bread and wine into the body and blood of Christ, a transmutation accomplished through the priest (as instrumental cause) pronouncing the historic words of Christ with the intention of consecrating the elements. But after that is said, the similarity between the Mass and the Last Supper, or between the Mass of today and the Mass of the first centuries, seems to stop abruptly. "The bread and wine don't bother me much," remarked a young professor attending instruction classes in a Phoenix parish, "but when I come to those vestments, I seem to lose touch with the simplicity of Jesus as described in the Bible."

There is seemingly little simplicity to the Mass ritual and the gorgeous panoply of vestments, ranging from pale rose through rich emerald greens for Sunday Mass to fiery crimsons for martyrs. An understanding of how the Mass got the way it is now often helps us appreciate it more, and to distinguish its changeless essence (the consecration) from the surrounding accidents of ceremonial and dress. There is (or was) a reason for everything; often, where something has lost its purpose (e.g., candles), a symbolic meaning has been attached to make up for the lost usefulness and to assist us to focus our thoughts on what is taking place before us: the Son of God is paying the debts of humanity by an unbloody, mystic death.

The vestments were originally the "Sunday best" of imperial Rome. When street clothes changed in style and started getting shorter, the Church retained the older style, and it remains in use to this day. The alb was a tunic, the amice a scarf or neckcloth, the chasuble (from *casula* meaning little house) a replica of the Roman *paenula* which had supplanted the Roman toga. The stole's origin is uncertain, but the maniple, small garment pinned to the priest's left arm, was originally a fancy-dress handkerchief! Priests often used it to mop their brows in summertime heat. The cincture originally kept the tunic (now the alb) in place.

Why vestments? Obviously they aren't necessary. The Mass can take place (and often does) without them. Their purpose is to be found in our natural instinctive response to color and beauty. It was this factor in us Christ appealed to when He gave us the sacraments with their *sensible* signs. Certainly the Mass is no ordinary action; hence the priest wears no ordinary clothes. Moreover as priest he is a kind of "universal man" acting as representative for mankind. The vestments detach him from any particular clime or nation or people, as Christ had detached Himself from any particular race or country by permitting Himself to be stripped of His clothes on the cross. Symbolic meanings are attached to the vestments to help us keep aware of the Mass's identity with Christ's passion and death. For instance, the amice is said to represent the cloth which the Roman soldiers used to blindfold Christ; the alb is a symbol of purity; the cincture recalls the cords that bound Christ to the scourging pillar; the maniple is a symbol of good works; the stole reminds us of our due obedience to Christ's yoke of providence; the chasuble reminds us of the purple garment in which Jesus was wrapped as He stood before Pilate.

The Mass is special, altogether special. Small wonder the priest who consecrates should wear special clothes and offer it in a special place according to special rubrics of ceremony.

The first Mass took place at the Last Supper, "on the night when he was being betrayed" (1 Cor. 11:23). The complicated ceremonial surrounding the consecration then was that of the Jewish Paschal dinner. It involved the eating of bitter herbs and unleavened bread, four fillings and quaffings of a cup of wine, the eating of the paschal lamb, plus prayers and benedictions and song. After that first Mass, further offerings of Mass down to our own time departed altogether from the paschal meal ceremonial. Even in the New Testament accounts of primitive Masses, the lack of detail regarding the ceremonial of the Mass is regarded as an indication that the paschal setting was not repeated.

But the Mass was early connected with a meal, the *agape*, at which free food was available to the Christian poor and a spirit of unity and harmony was inculcated. When some guests at these banquets refused to share their victuals and even got drunk on the wine, the consecration of bread and wine done by the priest at his table often passed unnoticed. Bitterly St. Paul condemns such abuse (1 Cor. 11:17-34).

The Church grew, and the room in which the Mass was offered was enlarged, only the celebrant's altar (table) was left, the agape disappeared, its last vestiges fading out in the fourteenth century.[9] The prayers at the foot of the altar gradually were transformed from silent prayers, said either in procession to the altar or during early incensations of it, into a public avowal of unworthiness. Around 1050 the *Confiteor* made its appearance in the form of various protestations of unworthiness and pleas for pardon. Though privately made at first en route to the altar, the protests of unworthiness became a formula publicly recited at the foot of the altar steps. (Psalm *Judica me* was made a general rule by the Missal of St. Pius V.)

In accord with ancient religious practice, the priest kisses the altar first thing on arriving there, for this is the spot where the greatest act on earth will take place. Then the priest reads the *Introit,* formerly sung by a choir while the clergy made their long way through the church and into the sanctuary. The conclusion, "Glory be to the Father and to the Son and to the Holy Ghost," was introduced as a battle cry against the Arian heretics of Antioch. They had substituted the ambiguous formula, "Glory be to the Father through the Son in the Holy Spirit," in which they bolstered their view that the Son is subordinate to the Father.

Sometime in the fourth century the people in the churches used to hear read a list of petitions and some would reply to each, *Kyrie eleison,* Lord have mercy on us. This "litany" was gradually incorporated in the Mass in various forms, including the simple repetition of the *Kyrie,* as early as St. Gregory the Great (ca. 540: Pope 590–604).

In the early days of the Church many individuals composed their own hymns, on the pattern of the psalms, called *psalmi idiotici.* Most of these songs are lost. One that has survived

---

[9] Jungmann, *op. cit.,* I, 17, footnote 44.

is the *Gloria in Excelsis Deo*. Though written and sung at first as a thanksgiving hymn (like the present-day *Te Deum*), the *Gloria* had by the sixth century become a regular part of the Mass.

Periodically in the Mass, like an alarm clock as Monsignor Knox put it, the priest turns to the people and says, *Dominus vobiscum*. It can be compared to the refrain "Now hear this," issuing from the loud-speakers of a ship of the U. S. Navy. Its aim is to get attention for the message about to follow. The message that follows this first "Now-hear-this," is that of the Oration or Collect. It sums up the character of the Mass prayers for each particular day, and its importance as a source of truth and spiritual insight is evident from an early prescription that the clergy and people kneel down for short prayer before it was read (*Flectamus genua*).

For a long time the celebrant ad-libbed his prayers just as he did his sermons to the people. Sometimes a less well-educated celebrant committed solecisms to the people's chagrin or merriment, and St. Augustine, for one, reminded them that good diction is less important at Mass than in the forum. From the third to the sixth centuries many of our present orations were composed, and the celebrant read them instead of extemporizing his own. The term "collect," Father Jungmann says,[10] takes its origin from the priest's "collecting" the people's prayers and, in the oration, presenting them to God.

The Mass gives us the Word of God made flesh in His bodily presence in the Eucharist. But it also gives us the Word of God embodied in concepts and ideas and clothed in words. Hence the fittingness of the epistle and gospel readings from Scripture. They hearken back to the practice of the Jews worshiping in their synagogues, who read passages each Sabbath

---

[10] *Ibid.*, p. 361.

day from the Old Testament, until it was all read, and then the cycle was repeated. The *Deo Gratias* at the end of the Epistle is less a spoken thank-you for the privilege of reading God's inspired message than an exuberant hurrah! or shout of approval; perhaps it originated in the great North African church.

Sandwiched between Epistle and Gospel are the Gradual and Alleluia (replaced by the Tract in Penitential seasons like Lent). The Gradual was originally chanted by deacons, then subdeacons, from one of the steps of the stairway leading to the ambo (raised desk). The Latin word for "step" is *gradus*; hence this chant came to be called the "Gradual."

Last of all the readings is that from the Gospels. Always the Gospels were honored most of all the inspired books, and presented in elaborately styled manuscripts bound in gold and silver and ivory. Only a priest or deacon must read it, and then in a special position of honor. Afterward the book is kissed. Candles and incense are other signs of honor to God's word. The making of a small sign of the cross on forehead, mouth, and breast (and by the priest on the book), dating from the eleventh century, is a triple reminder that those who read and hear the divine message of joy must first practice, then preach or read. Otherwise their role is automatic, like that of the bell in the steeple that clangs deafeningly and alone fails to hear its own brassy summons.

After His quadragesimal fast, Christ returned to Galilee and began to preach in the synagogue prayer services on Saturdays (cf. Lk. 4:14 ff.). After standing and reading the pertinent day's passage, He would sit and expound what He had read. What homilies those must have been! "His praise was on all men's lips" — at least at first (in verse 15); later (verse 29), the people tried to murder Him!

The custom of preaching on the Word of God is as old as the Church itself — and older. It was a part of the Jewish worship, and Jesus took advantage of it to turn a few sods in human hearts for the building that was to be His Church. It has always been a part of the Mass, sometimes occurring after the Gospel (as now), after the *Orate fratres,* after the reception of the offerings. This privilege[11] fell at first to bishops chiefly. Sometimes (viz., in Alexandria, Egypt, after the fall of Arius) priests were forbidden to preach. Often the preacher, especially the bishop, was seated and the people stood (chairs or pews are a modern, and praiseworthy, development).

The point is plain: throughout the centuries a man (priest, bishop) who not only shares in the eternal priesthood of Christ but is a child of his own age interprets the inspired word of God in terms suited to the capacity of his hearers. Just as the Body of Christ takes form under the appearance of bread in *this* place for *this* congregation, so the Word of God is made present in these terms, explained in these ideas, garbed in these words, as the divinity had been united to humanity. And whether standing, sitting on the floor, sitting in a pew, or leaning on a cane, the faithful were again meeting Christ in the guise of something contemporary with themselves: in ideas and forms of expression. This has ever been the goal of Jesus, and it lies behind the enormous benefit of the Holy Eucharist. For there Christ becomes contemporaneous in the greatest sense, by actually being present, Body and Blood along with His divinity, now, here!

The *Credo* (also called "Symbol") made its first appearance in the records of the ecumenical Council of Chalcedon (451). Because it summed up the beliefs of two other earlier councils

---

[11] Recall the remark of St. Joseph Cafasso: "I do not preach because I have to say something, but because I have something to say."

(Nicea in 325 and Constantinople in 381) it is also called the Niceno-Constantinopolitan Creed, or more familiarly, the Nicene Creed. It was used at first as a statement of his belief to be made by the candidate for baptism. Hence the first person singular, "I believe." It found its way into the Mass by order of Patriarch Timotheus (511–517) of Constantinople, though placed earlier in the Mass than now, and this practice was adopted all over the East. By 589 it was said before the *Pater Noster* in Spain. Two centuries later it was in France and in the tenth century farther North. One interesting incident concerns the Emperor Henry II who was surprised to find no *Credo* in the Mass in Rome in 1014. The Pope explained that there was no need for it since there had been no heresy there to demand its presence in the Mass. But the Pope, Benedict VIII, finally gave in to the emperor's importuning and the *Credo* made its appearance on Sundays and certain great feast days. The music which presents the text of the *Credo* in High and Solemn Masses is some of the richest in the entire repertoire of church music.

In Genesis we already find people making songs and dances. From his primordial roots, man gathered within himself his hopes and loves and sent them wafting and surging toward God in torrents of song. The Mass, being perfect worship, has always made use of music. In fact, the Mass was for many centuries offered only as a sung Mass. The Low Mass, in which the Mass prayers are all *read*, is a later development, occurring together with the growth of the number of priests in the monasteries; they naturally wished to offer Mass daily, and the form in which they offered it was the simplified one of a Low Mass.

It used to be the custom for the people to bring their gifts and offer them to the priest during the Mass. This carrying up of the gifts was called the offertory procession. It took quite a while for all the people to troop up with their gifts of bread and wine, geese and hens, pots and pans, bedding, flax, sheaves of wheat, lambs, pigs, and what have you. So to occupy the congregation, a song was chanted; this was the offertory chant, performed by special singers. After the year 1000, when money began replacing the barter system of economy, the offertory procession naturally began to disappear when the people began wisely to give money instead of gifts of produce.

Today at a Papal Mass on the occasion of a solemn canonization there is an offertory procession in which are carried two breads, two barrels of wine and water, five candles, and three cages of pigeons, turtle doves, and other birds. But by and large the offertory procession has disappeared. And when it went, the long chant also disappeared. Instead, the priest reads only the antiphon which formerly was sung before and after the long chanted offertory. One Mass which retains a verse of the old, lengthy offertory prayer is the Mass for the Dead.

"I can't get worked up over the offertory," one businessman remarked. "What have I to offer? The altar boys take up some bread and wine and water. But I haven't anything to give." What a wonderful task it was to inform this man that he was dead wrong.

He has very much to offer!

Do we have anything to offer to God? Yes, an immense amount! The bread and wine are *your* gift. The chalice and other sacred vessels have been offered by *you* for use in the Mass. The altar was *your* gift. *You* built the church and outfitted it with lights, statues, windows, stations, shrines, and pews. The little altar boys didn't just materialize. They are *your* offering. Most of all! The priest — he is one of your sons.

You have nothing to offer? Rather, you have a vast amount to offer. You have *already* offered much. It is the priest alone who consecrates by his will and his words. But he needs *something* to consecrate. You gave it. And he needs his own life. You gave that. Your Christian home life nourished the beginnings of his vocation.

Nothing to offer! Nothing, except the whole visible apparatus of Christ's Church, product of your sweat and generosity. Nothing to offer except the example of your lives, lived in union with Christ in the Mass. Nothing to give but the virtues you see exemplified by Christ in the Mass.

You offer yourselves at the Offertory, too. Don't leave your problems and worries at home. We don't live in a vacuum sans the germs of worry and the atmosphere of anxiety and difficulty. And we don't pray in a vacuum either. Parents, bring to Mass your concern over your children, particularly those in the agony of adolescence. Husbands, bring to Mass your concern for your wife's health and for your work, your career, your family's future. Wives, bring to Mass your frustrations and discouragement, your weariness with the daily routine. Teachers, don't leave at home your anxiety over a backward or indifferent student. Bring it to Mass with you. All these things we can offer to God, along with ourselves, for they are a part of us. And they will be changed, when we are changed, in the Mass and Communion into more reasonable facsimiles of the living Jesus.

The *symbol* is beautiful: people marching up together visibly giving, giving together, to sustain the Holy Sacrifice. The *reality* is most important: people sustaining the Mass by their money gifts, their sacrifices, their lives, their children.

The washing of the hands is an ancient ceremony going back to the roots of Christianity. It may have been introduced into the Mass originally as a symbol of the purity required of priest and people to offer and attend Mass properly. Mingled with it, especially later, was the element of practicality. The priest, after handling the gifts of the people, must wash the dirt off before touching the body and blood of Christ.

The *Orate fratres,* though originally addressed to surrounding clergy, is nevertheless a clear sign of the whole people's part in the Mass. "Pray that my *and your* sacrifice be acceptable." Sometimes the fact that the priest makes a complete turn here is adduced as evidence of his desire to include *all* the people in his invitation to pray that the sacrifice be acceptable. The reason for this complete turn, as opposed to the half turns at other times, is perhaps to be found in the fact that the priest turns toward the side where the book stands from which he will read.[12]

The Mass belongs to you, the people, all of you. The Council of Trent said that Christ at the Last Supper left a sacrifice *to the Church.*[13] You are the living stones from which Christ's Church is made. The Mass belongs to you. It is not my Mass or the bishop's Mass: it is the Church's Mass. You take a part in it. True, the priest alone consecrates, and can consecrate though no one but himself is present. Yet even then the Mass continues to be the Church's sacrifice, and all the members of it are summed up in the Mass, offering and being prayed for by Christ.

The Secret (so-called probably because it was said in a very low tone, at least from around the middle of the eighth century) was formerly the only prayer said during the whole of the offertory ceremonial. There was a certain pattern: the Collect had concluded the great entrance procession of clergy;

---

12 Jungmann, *op. cit.,* Vol. ii, p. 85, footnote 25.
13 Deferrari, *op. cit.,* p. 288. Session 22, chap. 1 (Denz. 938).

the Postcommunion had concluded the Communion ceremonies; the Secret concluded the offertory activity. It asks,
always in the plural, that *our* offerings and ourselves might
be accepted by almighty God, that as bread and wine are
changed, we ourselves might be changed into something more
representative of Christ.

Within the Mass lies an area containing in itself the very
heart or essence of Christ's sacrifice. This area is called the
Canon (fixed rule, because it ended extemporizing by the celebrant), and the precious kernel it contains is the consecration,
most appropriately called the *"Actio,"* or Action. It is *the*
Action par excellence. It is not mere ceremonial trappings or
symbol-laden ritual. It is an Action performed by Christ, using
as instrument the priest.

The consecration is *the* Action of actions, a symphony of
the Real Presence produced by divine genius operating in
the human heart and will and words of a priest. Timeless,
universal bread and wine become the food God has prepared
for humanity. It is because of this divine *Actio* that the Mass
is more than merely "a beautiful play of symbols; its aim is
to effect a real union of the soul with Christ." The entire
Canon was once called the *Eucharistia* or thanksgiving prayer.
This note of thanks, of gratitude, is sounded long and loud
in the Preface at the outset of the Canon. Here, as often elsewhere, we remark that our praise and love and thanks go to
God via Jesus Christ. We express our thanks *before* the consecration *for* the Mass, and *after* it *through* the Mass. Our
hearts go upward to God and, at the consecration, the movement is reversed, from God to us, and it issues in the presence
before us of the Son of God Incarnate.

In a certain sense, the sanctification of every creature lies
in its being "turned into" Christ. A man "becomes" Christ

(= Christlike) by growing in grace and the virtues. The elements find their *conversio* by being a part of man and sharing through him in divine life. Bread and wine in the Mass are changed into the body and blood of Christ, and it is this change which makes the Mass something acceptable to God. He loves the soul in which He sees Himself reflected in the virtues; He is satisfied with the Mass because in it He sees the sacrifice of His Son present there. Beauty often induces gasps of delight and phrases of astonishment. The greatest beauty usually is met in stunned silence, unbelieving muteness. When the *Sanctus* bell rings, it draws down a curtain of silence as ornament for the consecration that is on tap. Since the fifth century the Church has immersed its most Sacred Action in this prayerful silence. As if to say: what happens here is of the heart and mind of man, not of brawn and violent force, working a transformation in bread and wine, ultimately in the soul of humanity, as subtly as yeast breathes dimension into bread. Here is where the great, the lasting changes occur.

What is it that makes the Mass the Mass? The answer, by authority of the Council of Trent, is the consecration. Christ in the consecration is the real Gift that is offered to God; the consecration is the moment of actual sacrifice, the climax, over and over again in our lives as in Christ's, of human experience. Now that it is over in the Mass, the people don't walk out, any more than they leave a play when the climax has taken place. The denouement remains. In a play, the threads of the plot must be tied up; in the Mass, Christ must enter into us in Communion.

The *Unde et memores* prayer, right after the consecration, indicates that in the Mass we have present the Christ who not only suffered and died (and is suffering and dying mystically upon the altar) but also the Christ who arose from the dead

and ascended into heaven (and is rising and ascending to inter-
cede mystically upon the altar). Christianity is a religion for
"opti-mystics," ending as it does not on the sorrowful note of
death and burial but with the triumphant ringing exclamation
of resurrection. This, too, is contained in the Mass in the presence of the risen Christ.

The *Memento* (or remembrance) of the Dead, which appeared in the Mass prayers as early as the fourth century, not
only signifies the ability of the Mass to reach across the boundary
of death in aid of souls but allows the celebrant and people
to apply the endless profits of the Sacrifice to souls special to
them. The dead have not dropped from the list of members of
the Church; they are not relegated to an inferior order. They
have triumphed, whether they are in heaven or in purgatory.

For centuries in the early Church clerics used to add the
word "sinner" to their signatures. This practice seems to have
been incorporated into the Mass prayer in the *Nobis quoque
peccatoribus*. The "sinners" referred to here are especially the
priests on whose frail shoulders so great a burden has been
placed. But almost immediately afterward priests, and all, remember that they are a part of Christ who acts in, with, and
through them to sanctify themselves and, through them, the
world. So the heavy burden can be carried, and with joy.

The Communion part of the Mass begins with the prayer
Pater Noster. How fitting! The prayers of the Church are au-
dacious. We address God as our Father. What a daring name
to give God. Pagans through aeons fell into one of two alterna-
tives: they brought God near to them by giving Him all the
qualities of humans, including their vices; or they kept pure
their idea of God but lost sight of Him as a force in their lives
in a haze of abstract ideas without appeal or sentiment to the
majority of people. In Christ this dilemma is resolved. In Him

we possess eternal, almighty God together with frail, time-bound man of clay, sans only sin. How aptly the word "Father" brings the Almighty into our hearts dearly and nearly. How otherwise could we dare to tell God, as we do in the hymn *Attende, Domine,* to *wake up* and be merciful to us? It is this same God, Father, Son, Holy Ghost, who comes into our hearts in Communion. The intimate title "Father" invites the intimate Communion Guest.

According to ancient Jewish practice, bread for the meal was broken into smaller pieces just before being eaten. The name "breaking bread" came to mean "eating dinner." Now, just before Communion, the priest breaks the sacred Host, another sign of the continuity of Old and New Testaments, of Jewish and Christian faiths. It may well be that this rite originated in the custom of the early days for the Pope or some other bishop to send a particle (called the *fermentum*) of the Host from his own Mass to priests in outlying areas to drop into their chalices at Mass as a sign of the *unity* of the Mass in all places at all times, holding the whole Church together.

The *Agnus Dei* refers to the sacramental Christ, the Christ who was broken and bruised and is present now in the Eucharist. It used to be chanted while priests and deacons were busy breaking the consecrated Bread into particles small enough to be received by the people (this before the days of small, unleavened wafers). Historians of the liturgy note that the lamb was used more often in sacrifice than any other animal. Nowadays, the only sacrifice acceptable to God, the Mass, has the divine Lamb as its priceless Victim.

Priest and people enter, at this point, into the closest contact with God possible in this life, Holy Communion. Always religious sacrifice has involved ritual eating. Jewish priests in the Temple put aside choice steaks and chops from sacrificial animals. Eating them involved religious overtones. In the Mass we enjoy not just some viand smacking of religious worship; we consume God-made-man, body and blood, divinity, everything. Small wonder that the remaining prayers both derive their names from this union (Communion, Postcommunion prayers). In a real sense, Communion is so grand an event that every incident in our lives can be dated so many minutes, hours, and days after Communion.

If any event should induce ecstatic joy, Communion is it. Perhaps that is why the Church selected the opening of St. John's Gospel to accompany the Mass-goer on his way. This high-flying treatise of the loftiest mysteries of God closes out the epic half-hour of Mass. The verses were once read over the dying before receiving Extreme Unction, over the newly baptized, and even during stormy weather in hope of halcyon days of sunshine. Now they conclude (since at least A.D. 1256) the holy Mass, which comforts the heart sick, baptizes the disconsolate and weary with the blessings of peace and hope, and brings the sunny weather of God's divine comforts all through the year.

Loose Ends

DOCTOR G., a well-known surgeon and practicing Catholic in a town in South Carolina, had a "middle age upset." In the crisis of discovering that he was growing old and that the fulfillment of his old dreams had not meant what he thought it would, he began stepping out with his secretary, trying to "feel young." The secretary was one of those gold diggers who try to lure middle aged fogeys away from their duty when they begin to fear age and (as is common) assert their refusal to grow old despite a family growing up or grown. Dr. G. had nine children, two of them in college!

To the great disgrace of his family he "married" the young secretary and moved away. His heroic wife and mother of the nine children kept her wits and her faith, and prayed continually, especially at Mass. She had many Masses offered for his return to his religion and his senses.

The doctor, as a prominent surgeon, had no difficulty getting a position in a university hospital in another state. As the years passed, his family never stopped their prayers for him, and heard Mass after Mass for that intention. One afternoon on his way home from the hospital he had a heart attack and went into a coma. His "wife" called a priest. When the priest entered the sickroom, the doctor became conscious. After confession and the last sacraments, he again lost consciousness. He died two days later. "When I think of him," remarked one of the sons, "I'm very happy, because I know he's with God."

Such is the power of the Mass, to bring back souls from the very brink of total loss in hell. It ties up the "loose ends" of life, gathers up the stray sheep and the wandering lambs that no one ever guessed could or would come back.

Jesus' life must have seemed to the Apostles much like a loose end, unfinished, dangling, leading to nothing. Then His resurrection came and tied it into meaningfulness. The crucifixion looked to the Apostles, in their dismay, like a cul-de-sac. Did they perhaps wonder if they had been played a "dirty trick"? Christ's contemporaries could not see the forest of redemption for the three trees on Calvary.

In our own life, too, there are many loose ends. Perfectionists and others who try to knit them all in are bound to be frustrated, because only in heaven will all the frayed edges and the loose ties be brought together and seen as a meaningful part of the fabric of life. When a man dies, how many thousands of items we could classify as loose ends! Intentions unfulfilled, good undone, work started but never finished, goals never reached, dreams unrealized, friends unvisited. The keel of a great plan is laid but left incomplete amid the scaffolding of death. Ideas in throngs wait to become incarnate in the flesh of spoken and written words, only to be denied when genius flames out. But that is what life has to be!

Human life is not lived in tiny and neat compartments, each precisely and unequivocally identified and ordered. It is no Japanese tearoom garden of carefully raked sand and serene plantings of trees and shrubs. Life is rather the untamed jungle bristling with teeming, untrammeled things. It is the uncharted swamp with necklace of cattails and chorus of honking geese in serried squadrons. It is the undulant prairie spilling over a bent horizon, the shadowy gorges and peaks of mountain ranges, the pampas and wastes of ocean water!

Human life will be complete only in heaven. On earth there will always be unsolved puzzles, unwritten laws, unopened doors, unlocked mysteries, slighted love, fields unploughed, and harvests never reaped, scythes that gather rust, walls heaped like sinter around a gaping, weed-grown basement where once played the burning fountain of life.

Frustrated plans trademarked the saints. St. John Francis Regis, after a meteoric career among the peasants of France's Cevennes mountains, died while a letter in the pouch of a messenger hurrying to Rome sought his dismissal from the Jesuit order. Not all our plans find perfect fulfillment. Some founders of religious orders were later ousted from the orders they founded! This happened to Alphonsus Liguori, Blessed Teresa Couderc, Joseph Calasanctius, and Blessed Mary Teresa de Soubiran. Consider the case of the last mentioned.

Sophie de Soubiran la Louviere, born May 16, 1835, later founded the Society of Mary Auxiliatrix. An influential member of this society, Mother Mary Frances, by unwise schemes for its development, got it into financial tangles, and then blamed the foundress, who had taken the name of Mother Mary Teresa. On the advice of Father Paul Ginhac, Mother Mary Teresa resigned. Her successor was the very same Mother Mary Frances! By 1847, Mother Mary Teresa had been ejected from the order she had founded! (Her mother, one of the first to enter the congregation, was also thrown out.) She died June 7, 1889, of TB as plain Sophie de Soubiran. It did not make any difference to cheerful, long-suffering Sophie, now happy in heaven, that Mother Mary Frances turned out to be a married woman who had deserted her husband to become a nun; that her vows were invalid; that she was not mother general of the society, that she had never really expelled the foundress; that she was herself expelled in 1890 and lived 30 more years, long enough to see the beginning of the movement to canonize Sophie de Soubiran. That is the way life has to be.

There will always be unshed tears, unmoved mountains, unturned sod, unnamed fears. The teacher will see time and time again lessons unlearned, knowledge neglected, principles unpracticed. In national life, more loose ends: unchecked spending, unbalanced budget, inflation, depression, jobless workers, surplus farm goods destroyed or left to rot, crimes in many cases unpunished, some disloyal citizens, unrestrained ambition, relentless greed. These will always characterize our society and — an unconquerable spirit.

Life is not a great Gobelin tapestry with its finished, just-the-way-you-want-it loveliness. Instead, in every cranny of experience there are examples of the unfaithful husband or wife, the unloved child, unbridled passions, the traitorous apostle, the unjust steward, love unrequited, abandoned homes, abandoned hopes, springs of human kindness seemingly gone dry.

Even in the twilight years of life, unsteady steps are still falteringly pursuing unfulfilled wishes, and trembling, emaciated hands still grasp for goals unattained.

The Mass makes up for much of this incompleteness. It helps us see that one of life's properties is this very "unfinishedness." Franz Peter Schubert, who died in 1828, wrote a famous symphony called the *Unfinished Symphony*. Yet it was completed long before his death, and takes its name from its having two movements instead of the customary four. Life is like that. We think it is incomplete, not as we would like it, yet does this not lie rather in our view of life than in life itself? Our lives *can* be filled with beauty and the genius of piety, proclaims the Mass, if we will but draw from it resources of divine courage. Happiness, the Mass says, will not be found in the "customary" things. Divinity, Bishop Sheen once observed, is found where we least expect it: in a cave, in the lineaments of a helpless babe, in a corpse stiffening on a cross. It *will* be found in the will of God, as made known in the living newscast of daily experience.

Across the centuries, did David glimpse the Eucharist, when, in Psalm 104, he spoke of God's "subsidy of bread," bread which guards and defends and attacks the enemy, bread which gives succor and offers asylum from the dragnet of the implacable foe? The Eucharist-giving Mass is by all means a subsidy for poor human nature, hard up for the will and wisdom needed to keep God in sight through the years and the harrowing by time.

One of the most disturbing factors of human life is loneliness. A feeling of abandonment like a gloomy, interminable fog often settles into life, driving out the warmth and blotting out all view of the cheering horizon of hope. No one has more sensitively probed this area of nostalgic, lonely yearning for something out of reach and perhaps not even known than the novelist Thomas Wolfe. In *The Hills Beyond* Wolfe in his compelling prose flavored with an intense experience of life describes a man's return to a boyhood home in St. Louis. In that dimly recollected house a much loved brother had died years ago. And now the surviving boy has returned, no longer a boy but a man of 42, and searching. He remembers the name of the street, Kingshighway of magic memory, a gabled, turreted roof, and a backyard plot of grass. He finds the house, but so much smaller and less regal than he remembered it. There in the backwash of a dying afternoon he learns at last that you *can't* go home again, that the past is done, and his heart cries out somewhere for driftwood of hope to cling to in the inexorable ebb-and-flow of scabrous time. In a rare piece of mild polemic, Wolfe, recalling this piercing experience, said that the central purpose of Christ's life was "to destroy the kingdom of loneliness and establish in its place the kingdom of love."

Wolfe has hit upon it. Christ *does* destroy loneliness. Especially by His tender consolation offered in the Mass. One of life's loose ends is this very loneliness, a feeling so keen it inspired some of Thomas Wolfe's most poignant passages, enchanting lines that will ever ring the bell of human experience. The Mass ties up this loose end by giving us the loving Guest, Jesus in Holy Communion. In Him is found the fellowship the human heart is seeking.

A few years ago the *London Daily Sketch* ran a series of articles under the general heading, "If Christ Came Back." One contributor allowed He would be enmeshed in politics. Billy Graham said there was no "if" to it: He will come back. (Theologians call this second coming of Christ the "parousia.") Father Joseph Christie, S.J., had the last and best word. "The question about our Lord coming back," he wrote, "is interesting but academic. He has never been away. In any Catholic Church you can find Him, and His authentic voice goes down the ages through His teaching Church."

The Mass ties up the loose ends. Christ the Priest comes in the Mass "to perfect all who were to be sanctified, and bring them to fulfillment."[1] This is the fulfillment Wolfe strove for in vain. This is the bond making all men brothers despite the wars and hates that threaten to atomize the familyhood of man. At Mass the whole Church is at work, offering the love of its heart to God by a profound and spontaneous movement, in the person of Christ the Head, who operates in and through His priest.[2]

The blurred faces whipping by as the *Super Chief* powers through Flagstaff en route to Chicago, the lonely fisherman standing on a dike with cane pole in hand, the figure at the frozen window on a wintry night waiting, all these are *truly* united in love and adoration in the Mass.

The Catholic instinctively looks to the Mass to patch up the frayed edges worn by loneliness on the wilted collars of his days. An ex-junior-grade lieutenant who served four years in the Navy during World War II has seen deeply into the Mass. He wrote: "No matter where I went, the Mass more than anything else kept me linked up with all that is valuable in life. The Mass kept me in touch with the people, the ideas and ideals, the realities that are so easily lost sight of in the relative anonymity of service life. Somehow, everywhere I served, I managed to find a church and get to Mass pretty regularly. Once near Alexandria, Egypt, I ended up in a poor

---

[1] *The Church Teaches*, p. 291 (Denz. 747).

[2] Cf. address of Pius XII to the 1st International Congress of Pastoral Liturgy, Vatican City, Sept. 22, 1956.

wooden box of a church filled with raggedy-ann people singing a weird chant. They were accompanied by the jangle of cymbals and an exotic flute. Yet even there, surrounded by a strange, and mysterious ritual, I felt at home. After all, I was at Mass."

"That's where a Catholic is most at home — at Mass."

The Mass is high point of union with God on earth, especially when at Mass we receive Holy Communion. The Mass is not just the gift-giving stage of friendship with God, but a consummation; it is what gift-giving is meant to lead up to. A Jesuit missionary who worked among American Indian tribes remarked, "The tribes I worked among had a custom when a bargain was to be made or an agreement reached, and in former days when a treaty was to be drawn up, of going through a gift-giving ceremony. They smoked the peace pipe and exchanged belts of wampum." A highlight of the lives of the North American martyrs took place around Iroquois and Algonquin campfires, when the smoke-stung, snow-blinded blackrobes matched tribal orators word for word in lavishing formal gifts and ceremonial benisons. Such was the custom of these peoples, grippingly recounted in the *Jesuit Relations*.

When we wish to ingratiate ourselves with others, we ply them with gifts. King Saud and ex-President Eisenhower exchanged presents when the Arabian monarch visited America. Queen Elizabeth II and Prince Philip of England, on their good-will mission to the United States in October, 1957, gave Ike a pair of American parula warblers sculpted in porcelain and a coffee table inlaid with a map of the President's Normandy invasion strategy. He in turn gave the royal pair a ceramic sculpture of the prince in polo regalia and a portrait he had painted of their son Prince Charles.

A young man and woman often exchange gifts in order to establish a friendship or repair a damaged one. Companies

179

send gifts to employees and customers at Christmas time. Politicians have been known to shower largesse on voters in election years. Candidate Carlos P. Garcia, elected president of the Philippines to succeed much mourned Ramon Magsaysay, passed out Garcia buttons with ten-peso bills folded inside. His object: to make friends with the voting populace. He and his principal rival Jose Yulo ran up a bill of some $13 million in catering to ballots in 1957.

When friendship is at a certain unripe stage, gift-giving is introduced to mature and ripen it, as God's gifts of rain and sun ripen wheat. The Greeks' gift of a huge wooden horse to the Trojans did not mark the consummation of the warring people's friendship-in-reverse. The climax came later, when the warriors clambered out of their hiding places in the great carved beast and captured startled, sheepish Troy. Publishers make gift copies of dictionaries and textbooks to college and university professors, not as the culmination of an association but rather as its overture. Stores at grand openings dispense shiny new merchandise in give-away sales in hopes of inaugurating long and mutually-beneficial friendships.

In each case, the gift-giving stage is not the zenith but a preliminary step to more intimate union and friendship, in which riches are shared more liberally. The mutual sharing that follows gift-giving is not so much a gift-exchange as a transfer of good will and love in a more advanced state of reciprocal friendship and love. The courtship of our fathers and mothers involved various degrees of gift-giving, with the gifts getting more expensive; finally there came a sharing of a common life and destiny and fortune, their table and all their hopes, and life itself.

Now the Mass is the stage of union with God, rather than the gift-giving stage. The gift-giving stage is the preliminary arrangement, when we give our attention to and keep the commandments; when we give our allegiance in baptism; when we offer fuller and more complete dedication of ourselves in confirmation; when in confession we reform and rededicate ourselves; when in the length and breadth of our life we give God service in the practice of the virtues in imitation of the "new commandment" Christ gave.

Finally in the Mass we share a higher function and perform along with Christ the great sacrifice of adoration, thanksgiving, reparation, and petition; we unite with Christ, and all members of His Church, in offering the profound act of union with God, the Mass. It is a God-and-man function of the highest order. The priest-celebrant alone offers the sacrifice; but those present can and ought to take a reverent part by offering Jesus to His Father by union of wills (through love), by union of action (through sacrifice in daily living and by contact with the "action" of Christ in the Mass), by union of minds (through contact with the truth-funneling elements of the Mass). The Mass gives both grace and truth, life and unity.[3]

And of course we share the sacred table with God, and the overflowing of sanctifying grace. In perfect attendance at Mass we do not merely *say* we are united with God. We *mean* it. "Giving our will" to God means uniting with God. And the way we unite with God is by means of our will, in love and obedience.

"Father, the Mass seems like a detour to me," said a jet pilot stationed at Forbes Air Station, near Topeka, Kansas. "I know that we want the love of God. But instead of 'pure love of God' we get the Mass. Wanting the love of God, I can't help but be puzzled that I have instead a sacrifice with

---

[3] Pope Pius XII's address at the Assisi Liturgical Conference, Sept. 22, 1956.

181

so many rites and ceremonies. Why not go *directly* to God in pure love, without all the outward ritual?" Others express a similar notion when they say: "I will go out into the fields and woods, under the open sky, looking up into the starry expanse of space, and commune with God." That is a good idea, and it can be done with profit by most people at times. But in addition to, or rather foremost among, these ways to actually *commune* with God is the Mass and Holy Communion.

The fact that we go after the love of God in an indirect way — and attain it that way *most certainly* and *in the greatest abundance* — is not altogether strange. For in our ordinary life there are similar procedures. We want honor, so we go after learning, which will bring us honor. We want to play beautiful sonatas and concertos, so we practice endless scales and arpeggios. We want to be a champion boxer, so we skip rope to toughen our leg muscles and give us expertness and agility in footwork, or run for miles to build up our stamina. We want to be a diplomat, so we memorize grammar rules of languages. We want money, so we go out and look for a job. We want work, so we make friends with someone who can give us a job. We want to be a doctor of medicine, so we study physics and chemistry. We want to pray so we practice mortification in order that our prayer will be effective. We want to be exalted by God, so we humble ourselves. The martyrs lost their lives for Christ, and found them. The Little Flower of Jesus wanted to do great missionary deeds, so she retired to a convent and became the patron of missions along with St. Francis Xavier.

So there is rime and reason in our wanting the love of God and going to Mass to get it. The work of redemption was God's giving His love to us, primarily as that love is incarnate in the Person of Jesus. It is the Mass's job to "perpetuate the

182

work of the Redemption."[4] Hence we will increase the "pure love of God" best at Mass. It is no detour; it is God's own specially engineered superhighway bringing souls by the swiftest, most direct route to Himself.

The death penalty leveled on Jesus made His brief public career appear to be a loose end. Yet death served God's purpose, not God death's. Our lives, too, may sometimes seem "at loose ends," with dead ends of frustration, insoluble labyrinths of opposition and suffering, the aimlessness of good intentions thwarted, and hopes apparently ignored. Death, by Christ's wish, will also serve our purpose: death to sin and imperfection, death by the slow evolution of our lives to Christ-images, death like His own on the cross of our duty. Then we will see how everything has purpose, even pain, even failure. Then God will show us His master plan, the incomprehensible technological perfection of His wisdom, and His flawless Providence.

Until then, the Mass teaches these truths in a thousand ways, showing that nothing is wasted, nothing lost on God, and that our dream *can* materialize, and the noblest dream of all: to find perfect fulfillment in the satisfaction of our finest and holiest aspirations: loving intimacy with God.

---

[4] *The Church Teaches*, p. 297, translation of *Mediator Dei*.

INDEX

INDEX

La Colombière, Bl. Claude, 27
Lakhumara, hymn of thanks, 20
Lamy, Jean Baptiste, 74
Leoni, Pierre, S.J., 86 ff
Liebknecht, Wilhelm, 71
Lincoln, Abe, 7
Lindanus (William van der Lindt), 46
Liturgy, 132
Louis IX, St., 19

Machebeuf, Joseph, 74
Manor Bread Company, 56
Maritain, Jacques, 72
Martindale, C. C., S.J., 107
Martineau, Edward R., O.S.B., 136 ff
Marx, Karl, 71
Mass, aid to mental health, 122 ff; ceremonial development of, 159 ff; as debt payment, 11 ff; as gift exchange, 179 ff; utility of, 137
McCarthy, Raphael, S.J., 36
McKenzie, John L., S.J., 110
Mill, John Stuart, 42
Motivation research, 77

Nadal, Jerome, S.J., 141
Nature as purification, 24

Offertory procession, 163
Ormandy, Eugene, 115
Overman, Conleth, C.P., 35

Peace, given by the Mass, 32
Peking man, 17
Perseverance, 68 ff
Personal value, consciousness of, 39
Peter Canisius, St., 46
Petition, 26 ff
Pevensey, 1
Philip Neri, St., 45
Preaching, 162
Priest, fatherhood of, 113
Priesthood, need of, 100 ff
"Private" Mass, 103
Profit motive in virtue, 47 ff

Psychiatry and the Mass, 119 ff
Psychoanalysis, 129

Reparation, 22 ff
Rheims, Battle of, 9
Richard of Chichester, 37
Rouault, Georges, 72

Saints, long lives of, 134
Scheeben, Matthias, 41, 44
Scriptures, reading at Mass, 35
Sherwood, Tom, 18
Sibelius, Jean, 75
Signs of sacraments, 108 ff
Simon, André L., 59
Sin, effects of, 22
Sisk, John, 77
Sophie de Soubiran, Bl., 174
Spiritual Exercises, 127
Stein, Edith, 71
Stemper, Robert, S.J., 148
Suarez, Francis, S.J., 143
Suhard, 103
Sullivan, Harry Stack, 44

Tea ceremony of Japan, 148 ff
Thanksgiving, 19 ff
Tourism, 68
Trierweiler, Zeb, 97 ff

Utilitarianism, 29

Vestments, origin of, 157
Vogeler, Robert A., 105
von Cochem, Martin, 138

Weaver, Richard, 151
Will to fail, 36
William the Conqueror, 2
Wilson, Charles E., 72
Wine, nature of, 60 ff
Wolfe, Thomas, 177
Words of consecration, efficacy of, 104

Zhukov, 104

186